"This [is] an important book because it's about making wise choices. [*Choices of Champions*] is not just for the athlete. It's for the teenager, the housewife, the teacher, the mentor, the businessman, or the states-woman. The stories of Betsy King, Tiger Woods, Paul Bondeson, and Linda Armstrong Kelly not only warm the heart, but also have the power to change the heart. Once absorbed, these choices will become one of the greatest gifts you've ever given yourself. Give this book to someone you love or someone facing adversity, and it may well become one of the greatest books he or she will ever possess."

GARY PLAYER
Pro Golfer

"Paul Meier and Jim Hiskey have fashioned a remarkable tapestry of tragedy and triumph, pain and possibility, in the pages of this work. They teach us not only how to survive, but also how to thrive when the disappointments of life overtake us. This remarkable book will be a gift to many when dreams are crushed, ambitions frustrated, and goals unachieved. Read, cherish, and apply the timeless lessons of faithfulness, endurance, and perseverance contained in these wonderful pages."

JOHN A. WEBER
Dallas Cowboys Chaplain

"Jim Hiskey and Paul Meier have packed *Choices of Champions* with life lessons on becoming a champion. We read of famous athletes and everyday people who made difficult choices which led to extraordinary lives, inspiring us to examine our lives honestly, make the necessary changes, and become champions as well. Read and be challenged by this gem of a book!"

FRANCINE RIVERS
Author

"Jim Hiskey has been my close personal friend for nearly twenty-five years. He is someone I trust completely and whose heart is as close to always being in the right place as a human being can get. His life as a competitor, father, husband, friend, and minister have given him the perspective necessary to write this book and provide what all men have a need to hear. I believe in Jim and what he stands for."

TOM LEHMAN
PGA Tour Pro, Former British Open
Champion, and Ryder Cup Captain

"This is a deeply moving account of the life stories of individuals who overcame great obstacles—including severe accidents, self-destructive emotional illnesses, and even terminal disease—to make their lives meaningful and constructive. Many, but not all, are well-known athletes. Clinical insights into the resources they draw on—including their faith—make the book difficult to put down."

ARMAND M. NICHOLI JR., M.D.
Clinical Professor of Psychiatry,
Harvard Medical School

"I could not put this book down! Each of the lively, compelling stories drives home the fact that the choices we make, large or small, shape our lives and have an impact on those within our spheres of influence. The fascinating encounters with ordinary people who make extraordinary accomplishments redefine for me the meaning of a champion. *Choices of Champions* is nourishment to the soul!"

DR. CHARLES BALCH
Professor of Surgery and Oncology,
Johns Hopkins Medical Institutions

"When Ken Blanchard and I wrote *The Mulligan*, we created a wise 'Old Pro.' My Old Pro is Jim Hiskey, who has been my spiritual and writing mentor for thirty-five years. Jim and Dr. Paul Meier have brilliantly conceived and written *Choices of Champions*. Anyone who reads these heart-moving stories and makes the choices of true champions will be elevated to new heights of life."

WALLY ARMSTRONG
Former PGA Tour Player, PGA Life
Member, and Coauthor of *In His Grip*

"Everyone must read this book! It's a masterpiece in a hundred pages. We all have dreams and long to be free, but we get so entangled in life that we lose our way. These stories will help you find your way back."

ANN KIEMEL ANDERSON
Author of *I'm Out to Change My World* and *Seduced by Success*

"The book is fascinating and enlightening. This book is a great example of becoming a champion in life."

BERNHARD LANGER
Two-Time Masters Champion and
European Ryder Cup Captain

"Jim Hiskey and Paul Meier have written an uplifting book that tells the inspiring stories of those who are famous and those who are not. Whether you are a scratch golfer or have never picked up a club, you'll enjoy this book."

CHRISTINE BRENNAN
USA Today Columnist and
Author of *Best Seat in the House*

CHOICES OF CHAMPIONS

PAUL MEIER, M.D.
and JIM HISKEY

Tyndale House Publishers, Inc., Carol Stream, Illinois

Visit Tyndale's exciting Web site at www.tyndale.com

TYNDALE and Tyndale's quill logo are registered trademarks of Tyndale House Publishers, Inc.

Choices of Champions: 8 Critical Decisions Winners Make to Power through Adversity

Copyright © 2007 by Paul Meier and Jim Hiskey. All rights reserved.

Previously published as *Winning Is a Choice,* hardcover edition, by Tyndale House Publishers under ISBN-13: 978-1-4143-1280-4 / ISBN-10: 1-4143-1280-6.

Choices of Champions, softcover edition, first published in 2009.

Cover photo by Stephen Vosloo copyright © by Tyndale House Publishers, Inc. All rights reserved.

Author photo of Jim Hiskey copyright © 2006 by davidhartcorn.com. All rights reserved.

Designed by Jessie McGrath

Unless otherwise indicated, all Scripture quotations are from the *Holy Bible,* New Living Translation, copyright © 1996, 2004. Used by permission of Tyndale House Publishers, Inc., Carol Stream, Illinois 60188. All rights reserved.

Scripture quotations marked NIV are taken from the *Holy Bible,* New International Version®. NIV®. Copyright © 1973, 1978, 1984 by International Bible Society. Used by permission of Zondervan. All rights reserved.

The Library of Congress has cataloged the original edition as follows:
Meier, Paul D.
  Winning is a choice: how the champions do it, and how we can too / Paul Meier, Jim Hiskey.
    p. cm.
  Includes bibliographical references.
  ISBN-13: 978-1-4143-1280-4 (hc)
  ISBN-10: 1-4143-1280-6 (hc)
  1. Success—Religious aspects—Christianity. 2. Golf—Religious aspects—Christianity. 3. Sports—Religious aspects—Christianity. 4. Athletes—Biography. I. Hiskey, Jim. II. Title.
  BV4598.3.M45 2007
  248.8'8—dc22   2006037832

New repackage as *Choices of Champions,* softcover edition, first published in 2009 under ISBN-13: 978-1-4143-2008-3 / ISBN-10: 1-4143-2008-6.

Printed in the United States of America

15 14 13 12 11 10 09
 7   6   5   4   3   2   1

Dedication

I would like to dedicate my portion of this book to my sisters and brother, Bettye Lasesch, Nancy Brown, and Richard Meier. They have stuck by me all my life, through good times and hard times, with deep love and emotional and spiritual support. Each has been an inspiration to me as I observed their dependency on God to tackle life's obstacles. They have become "champions"—very successful and productive people. Thanks, Bettye, Nancy, and Richard. I love you.

★ *Paul Meier, M.D.*

Valna Hiskey, my mother, was a champion of champions. Misdiagnosed and in and out of the state hospital in Blackfoot, Idaho, she battled manic depression for fifty years. My dad, Peter Hiskey, was counseled by his attorney to leave her. Before my father died, I asked him why he stayed.

"I love her," he said. "I will never leave her." He didn't either.

My older sister, Beverly "Nina," arranged for Mom to see a doctor in Santa Rosa, California, who said, "Valna has been misdiagnosed." He gave her a new medicine that allowed her to live the last twenty-five years of her life as a normal, happy woman.

My sister was and is a true champion. When Dad was working and Mom was in the hospital, she and my older brother, Sonny, raised my younger brother, Babe, and me.

Babe, our great little brother, turned out to be the best golfer in the family, winning three times on the PGA Tour. He was a champion in the world's eyes as well as ours. And last but not least, I remember my older brother, Sonny, who was killed while on active duty in the air force. He taught us all to be fighters.

I dedicate this book to all of these special people. All champions. The best family a person could ever have.

Jan Hiskey

Table of Contents

Gary Player

Choices That Changed My Life

I believe this will prove to be an important book. But before I say why, I'd like to take you to my home in South Africa and tell you about a few choices I made that changed my life.

I grew up in a poor family near Johannesburg. My dad was a good-natured, hardworking man. As a laborer for the Robinson Deep and Crown Gold Mine, he never earned more than four hundred fifty dollars a month to support our family of five.

Dad was a big, burly man, over six feet and two hundred pounds. His friends called him Laughing Harry because he had a boisterous laugh. He loved golf and played well.

My older brother, Ian, started me in golf when he whittled my first club out of a stick and taught me how to swing. But a passion for the game didn't come until Dad took me out to Virginia Park Golf Course for my first round. I parred the first three holes. I think I had sevens and eights in all the rest, but it didn't matter. After the first three, I was hooked.

Another passion was also born that day. I met a lass—the prettiest girl I'd ever seen—Vivienne Verwey, who was the daughter of a golf professional and a good golfer in her own right.

I'll say more about Vivienne later.

My mom was a gentle, loving woman who insisted on courtesy and good manners. Tucking me into bed each night, she taught me to pray. When I was eight years old, Mom died of cancer. She was only forty-four.

A short time after Mom died, Ian joined the army. My older sister, Wilma, went to boarding school and Dad worked long hours, so I was often home by myself after school. These were the loneliest moments of my life.

But I did make friends at school, and one day when I was fifteen, a few of us decided to jump into a compost pit about twenty feet by twenty feet in size. The pit looked like a sunken haystack, soft and fun to jump into. Fearlessly I took off headfirst, like a high-diver. The moment my head hit the leaves and grass, I heard a loud *snap!* Lightning-like pain shot through my shoulders and into my head, and that was the last thing I remember. I was out cold.

I woke up in the hospital with a broken neck. I was afraid that I might end up as a quadriplegic and that my dreams of ever playing golf were pointless. Fortunately, however, the damage was reparable and I was eventually able to return to the sport I loved.

I practiced hard and learned as much as I could from Vivienne's father, Jock Verwey. But I had a difficult time with my swing; I often hooked the ball to the left. People said I was too small and my golf swing was too poor for me to ever amount to anything in the golf world.

But both Dad and Ian admonished me never to give up. One day after a particularly bad day at the course, I said, "Dad, I don't think I can become a champion. I'm too small. I can't hit the ball far enough."

My dad, though jovial, could be stern at times. This was one of them. "Laddie," he said, "listen to me. That's nonsense! It all depends on guts. *It's what's inside that matters. Not what's outside!*"

Dad's words and a movie I saw about this same time both had a great impact upon my life. The movie was the story of the greatest golfer in the world, Ben Hogan. Hogan was also a small man, about my size in fact, about five foot seven, one hundred fifty pounds. Hogan, too, had suffered a near-fatal accident, but he overcame both his size and the car accident to win more major championships than anyone who had ever lived up to that time.

As I walked out of the theater, I thought about what Hogan had accomplished. He had won the four major championships that make up the Grand Slam—the British Open, the Masters, the PGA Championship, and the U.S. Open. I knew then what I wanted to do with my life. *One day I will win those tournaments too,* I told myself.

Before I go on I would like to say something of the life-changing choices I made during my teenage years. As I reflect upon these years, I realize that I could have easily chosen to feel sorry for myself for losing my mother. Or for growing up in a poor family. Or for not having the opportunity to obtain a college education. Or for the fact that I was small. But I chose to accept my father's advice and believe that *it's what inside that matters, not what's outside.*

My brother was a soldier in World War II, and he taught me the importance of weight training and the benefits of physical fitness. I followed his example and used weight training to overcome my strength limitations. At that time, most pro golfers believed that bulky muscles were more a deterrent than a help. I chose to believe otherwise.

After I saw the movie about Ben Hogan I chose to follow my passion and become the best golf professional in the world. But I also told myself that if I didn't succeed, I at least wanted to become the best that I could be. Like Ben Hogan I began to practice intensely, eight to twelve hours a day, and improvement came rapidly. Before long, I was competitive with other South African pros.

After I turned pro and made my first good paycheck, I made another choice. I was eighteen when I chose to marry Vivienne. She has now been my beloved mentor and faithful companion for five decades, as well as the mother of our six children and the grandmother of our eighteen grandchildren.

Let me fast-forward to 1965.

It was a hot, sultry day in St. Louis, Missouri. I walked toward the seventieth green of the U.S. Open at the Bellerive

Country Club with a three-shot lead. I was now twenty-nine years old, and I had already won the British Open, the PGA Championship, and the Masters Championship. Only one of the majors had eluded my attempt to fulfill the dream I had had as an eighteen-year-old: the U.S. Open. An official marshal walked beside me and tried to encourage me. "You've got it locked up now," he said.

"No, don't ever say that. Not until that last putt is holed," I replied.

He meant well, but his words broke my concentration. I still had the lengthy par-three sixteenth and two tough finishing holes to play.

I regathered myself as I teed off, but my shot veered to the right and buried in the bunker. I blasted well past the pin and three-putted. Just as I pulled my ball from the hole, I heard the crowds roar on the seventeenth hole. My closest rival, Kel Nagle from Australia, had birdied.

My three-shot lead was gone.

At that moment, I had an important choice to make. Would I feel sorry for myself, would I blame the official for my three-shot loss, or would I regather myself?

It will do no good to be concerned about what's past, I told myself. *This is an opportunity to see what I'm made of.*

I parred the next two holes to get in a play-off, and the next day, I won the championship.

My childhood dream had come true. I had followed Ben Hogan. I had completed the Grand Slam by winning the four major championships. I was the third person in history, and the first foreign player, ever to do so.

Strangely, however, during the months that followed, I felt there was still something missing. I met with my friend and fellow pro Jim Hiskey at the Philadelphia Golf Classic shortly after my Open win and shared what I was feeling.

"I've won every tournament I've ever dreamed of," I said. "I've achieved all my goals, but I feel miserable. I have no purpose."

Jim listened and explained that what I was missing was spiritual purpose. I began to meet with a small fellowship of pros on Tour including Jim's brother, Babe; Paul Bondeson; Kermit Zarley; Dave Ragan; and Joel Goldstrand.

One year in Atlanta, Billy Graham spoke to our group. I stayed after the meeting and talked to Billy for some time. We became good friends, and over the years, he helped me discover a higher purpose in life.

In 1972, I was at the pinnacle of life.

Not only had I accomplished my childhood dream of winning the Grand Slam and married one of the finest women in the world, I also owned a home on one hundred acres of land. Zonnehoeve Farm, which is Dutch for "place in the sun," was located twenty miles from Johannesburg. We also owned Bellevive, a 1,500-acre studhorse ranch 250 miles north of Johannesburg. Vivienne and our children were all healthy and happy, and I'd just had one of my best years ever in professional golf.

At thirty-seven, I'd won eighty-six professional golf tournaments, six majors, nine South African Opens, and seven Australian Open Championships. I'd played golf with presidents, prime ministers, and CEOs of the world's largest companies. I'd also been received by the queen of England and presidents of the United States and South Africa.

I had a strong sense that I was serving a higher purpose. I had given back my U.S. Open prize money to help fund junior golf and fight cancer. Lee Elder, the first black golf professional ever to play in the Masters, accepted my invitation to come to South Africa. Together we conducted a number of golf events to demonstrate reconciliation between our races. I had also provided land and financial resources for two new schools for black children only a few hundred yards from my home. I had never felt more meaning and joy in my life than at the end of 1972.

But in January of 1973, the floor caved in.

Doctors in South Africa discovered that I had serious kidney problems and recommended immediate surgery. It took four of our continent's finest surgeons to repair the damage. The days that followed were the roughest of my life. After one week of lying in bed in agonizing pain, I doubted whether I would have any future in golf.

I yearned to leave the hospital and start practicing for the Masters in April, but my body was too weak to move. I hadn't missed the Masters in sixteen years, but doctors said I was not ready to play. Vivienne was expecting our youngest child at the time, and rather than lending her support, I could only receive consolation from her.

I thought a lot about faith, my purpose in life, my family, and what would happen if I couldn't play competitive golf.

During those three months I was determined to get well, but the days of my recovery seemed to drag. In early April I was finally able to begin a physical fitness program and felt a little stronger, but the gloom returned when the time of the Masters arrived. There I was in South Africa, barely able to move, let alone swing a golf club. Just the year before I had been confident that I could win again.

I realized that I might not ever play again. But almost as soon as the thought flashed across my mind, I remembered something that had happened twelve years earlier during the 1961 Masters Tournament. Tom Nieporte, my roommate, had given me a copy of Thomas à Kempis's *The Imitation of Christ* and asked me to read the chapter on adversity.

The words of Thomas à Kempis had reminded me of my father's advice that it's what's inside that matters. I had already come to believe that golf, as well as life, *was a journey in adversity*. But reading those words had reminded me that my adversities and trials were not what mattered most; what mattered was the way I reacted to them.

The next day I had won the tournament.

Looking back on that time, I realized that I wouldn't have won had I not chosen to accept adversity, face it head-on, and use it to motivate me to perform at a higher level.

By May, the gloom had disappeared. I returned to America and rejoined the PGA Tour. But as a result of my illness, I had lost much of my distance and was hooking the ball again. Even lessons from Jack Nicklaus and Lee Trevino didn't seem to help.

For the next seven weeks I persisted, but I played so poorly that there was no use going on. I headed back home, wondering if my career in golf was over. I spent the next month working on my ranch, chopping wood, getting plenty of exercise, playing with the children, and resting.

I now had another choice to make, a big one. I recalled that Bobby Jones and Byron Nelson retired early—gracefully. I found that I was happy on the farm, taking care of my growing stables of horses and having more time with my family. It would be no disgrace to retire.

But deep down I felt I could still win. I've made many choices in my life, but now in retrospect I believe this decision to accept adversity—in this case the surgery that brought me to the lowest level of my life—and see it as an asset was one of the most important choices of my life.

I chose not to retire, and I began to practice again.

Finally, I began to feel my strength and that familiar rhythm I had when I was playing at my best coming back.

I rejoined the Tour and shortly thereafter won the Southern Open in Columbus, Georgia, and the World Match Play in Britain.

When April 1974 arrived, I was ready for the Masters Tournament. I was grateful just to be playing. We never realize fully how much health and happiness mean until they are taken away.

Going into the last nine holes on the final day, I held a three-shot lead. Then Jack Nicklaus sank a fifty-foot putt for an eagle on the thirteenth hole to cut my lead to one. There are a hundred players I'd choose to have lurking behind me before I'd choose Jack Nicklaus! But on the seventeenth hole, my approach shot landed less than ten inches from the hole. A birdie, followed by a par on the last hole, secured my seventh major championship.

It has been a pleasure for me to write a few words at the onset of this book. I said earlier that I think this will be an important book because it's about making *wise* choices.

One of my favorite books is Proverbs, a book in the Bible written by Solomon for the purpose of helping readers become wise people.

Becoming a wise person results from wise choices.

As I look back on six decades as a professional golfer, I believe I never would have won nine majors on both the regular and Champions Tours, and 163 PGA events world-wide, or been elected into the Hall of Fame had I not made the choices I did.

Choices mean change, and change is often difficult. Our bodies resist the difficult and crave the comfortable. When I first came to America, I knew I did not have the distance I needed to compete with power hitters like Arnold Palmer. I chose to improve my physical fitness. A few years later, I won my first Masters. I laughed when I read that one reporter called me "Golf's Popeye."

If you come to my office in Palm Beach, Florida, you will see framed on the wall "My 10 Commandments of Life." The first one is probably the most important: "Change is the Price of Survival."

If I have learned anything in life it is that. Choosing to change, as Tiger Woods has shown us in recent years, is the path to becoming a champion in sports or in life. You will read about Tiger's changes on the pages that follow.

The choices I made as a teenager and in later years have shaped my entire life.

Obviously there was the choice to follow my passion and become the most fit and best golfer I could be. And the choice Vivienne and I each made to marry. There was the choice of following a higher purpose rather than just winning golf tournaments.

But the two less obvious choices—choosing to believe my dad's advice that *it's what's inside that matters most*, and choosing to accept adversity, face it head-on, and use it to motivate me to play better and live better—have been foundational for my life.

The other choices you will read about in this book are choices that can change a life. I've made them repeatedly.

This book is not just for the athlete. It's for the teenager, the housewife, the teacher, the mentor, the businessman, or the stateswoman. The stories of Betsy King, Tiger Woods, Paul Bondeson, and Linda Armstrong Kelly not only warm the heart but also have the power to change the heart.

Once absorbed, making these choices will become one of the greatest gifts you've ever given yourself.

Give this book to someone you love or someone facing adversity, and it may well become one of the greatest books he or she will ever possess.

Gary

Pro Golfer

Introduction

Choices Make Champions

Tiger Woods had dreamed of winning the U.S. Open since he was in grade school. He hadn't won in four tries as a young pro golfer, but in 2000, he was leading the tournament when disaster struck. Pushing his approach shot to the third green, the ball was so deep in the wirelike rough grass that it took him three shots to hack it out. Then he three-putted for a triple bogey.

As he walked off the green, Tiger Woods faced a choice that great champions make. Would he get hung up on his failure, or would he be able to move on?

Rachel lay over the steering wheel of her black Ford Explorer thinking the crash should have killed her.

She, too, faced a choice. Life and death depended upon that choice. Would she confront the reality of her situation and make a plan to improve it? Or would she give up?

Linda was seventeen years old when she got pregnant. Her boyfriend told her she could have the baby but not him. She hadn't graduated from high school. Her parents were poor and couldn't support her. She had no one to help her if she chose to have the baby.

She, too, faced a choice, and that choice would define her life. Would she sink into self-pity, or would she turn her obstacles into opportunities?

Paul Bondeson was one of the most talented young men ever to swing a golf club. Years later a freak accident paralyzed him from the neck down. He was told he would never have use of his arms and legs again.

Paul had a choice to make that day, a choice that could make him one of the great champions of life. Would he move into despair and self-pity, or would he choose to see a higher purpose in his situation?

Some of these people are athletes. Some are not. But all are *champions*—because of the choices they made at key moments of their lives.

1

WHY READ THIS BOOK?

My patients know me as a doctor. My readers know me as the coauthor of *Happiness Is a Choice* and *Love Is a Choice*. But few people know that I'm a sports fanatic. Most Sunday afternoons I'm sprawled out in my lounge chair, drinking diet cherry Cokes and watching a PGA tournament.

A couple of years ago I was offered an opportunity to play eighteen holes with a man who had competed in these tournaments. Jim Hiskey is a life member of the PGA and a former college all-American golfer. I was like a ten-year-old on his first trip to Disney World. I'd never played golf with a pro.

My excitement wore off fast.

After four holes, I'd lost three balls. I couldn't hit any club except a seven iron, which I used to drive with. I was in pain.

On the fifth hole, Jim had mercy on me. He changed my grip.

When I gripped the club on the fifth tee, I thought it would fall out of my hands. But even though changing my grip felt wrong, Jim's knowledge of golf made me think his counsel was right.

I made a halfhearted choice: I'd change my grip even though I had little faith anything would be different.

After I hit my five wood about 250 yards on the eighth hole—something I had never done—I began to think there might be something to Jim's advice.

My attitude changed. Even though I thought the shot was somewhat of a fluke, I knew that if I was going to improve my golf game, I had a choice to make. I could stick to my old way, or I could change to this new, strange way Jim was proposing. He had been a PGA pro for forty years, and I believed he was qualified to help me. That day he became my golf doctor, and I chose to risk change. I played one of the best rounds of my life.

I've wanted to write a book on this subject for many years. I've always been fascinated by champion athletes and wondered how they attain their success.

I've thought a lot about a different type of champion too. In my work as a psychiatrist, I see people who face many obstacles—abusive backgrounds, eating disorders, personality disorders, and so forth. Some never change, but others amaze me by finding a way to improve their lives.

How do they do it?

After playing golf with former PGA Tour pro golfer Jim Hiskey and discovering that he, too, was a writer, I suggested that we coauthor this book. Jim has a passionate desire to help men and women, young and old, skilled and unskilled, and his golfing background gives him perspective on athletic success.

We met in Dallas shortly thereafter, and after two days of brainstorming, we came to these conclusions:

- Becoming a champion in life, not merely in sports, is what really matters.
- A champion can be defined as someone who has climbed a hurdle and reached greater heights in life. It's someone who recognizes his or her gifts and chooses to use them to help others. Being a champion has to do with finding a higher purpose in life.
- Everyone can win in life. Some people honestly feel as if they are losers. But everyone can make the wise choices that lead to winning in life. Sometimes they simply need help to see what those choices are.
- Anyone can become a champion in life, even people who believe they are locked into an impossible situation.
- We can learn important lessons by closely observing the choices made by champions.

This is a book of stories about champions.

Jim's stories highlight champion athletes—mostly golfers, but also athletes from other sports. My stories describe some of the clients I've met in my years of counseling. Each story illustrates a choice that helped that individual overcome an obstacle and become a champion.

You, too, can become a champion. As Jim and I tell these stories, we hope you will consider how you can make similar choices. How can you overcome obstacles, discover your gifts, and live your life to its fullest potential? Will you decide to change? Will you make the choices of champions?

We have thoroughly enjoyed writing this book and have learned a great deal about making wise choices. It is our heartfelt hope that these stories will be enjoyable to you and will change your life as they have ours.

Paul Meier

2

THE BETSY KING STORY

Champions Choose to Accept Help from Others

After leading her team to the NCAA championship and winning low amateur honors at the United States Women's Open in 1976, Betsy King had dreams of one day beating all the pros and becoming the outright Open champion.

Immediately upon graduation from Furman University, the five-foot-six-inch blonde with the sweeping golf swing joined the Ladies Professional Golf Tour.

Four years later she was wondering if she'd made the right decision. She'd competed in more than one hundred tournaments without a win. A disappointed aunt told her, "Betsy, you've lost your competitive edge."

Betsy was disappointed too. She had worked hard, and her dreams of winning the U.S. Open—or any LPGA tournament—seemed more remote than ever. Resolved that she might not ever win, she thought, *Well, if I can't win, I'll be the best nonwinner I can be.*

In Betsy's fifth year on tour, Donna Horton White invited her to play in a team event in Portland, Oregon. That week Donna, an LPGA tournament champion and one of the pros that Betsy most admired, gave her some advice that would change her life and career.

"I've always been a hard worker," Betsy says now. "If someone had told me that I could win the U.S. Open if I hit a million practice balls, I would have hit a million practice balls."

But Betsy's work ethic hadn't been enough.

She'd received golf lessons as a youngster, but she saw no need for further instruction since she was a professional. At that time, 90 percent of the other LPGA pros didn't have a teacher either.

Donna countered this view. "She told me I should get a good teacher," Betsy says. "She had someone in mind: Ed Oldfield, a respected golf instructor from Portland."

Though Betsy had some misgivings about asking Ed to help her, she thought so highly of Donna that she decided to meet with Ed and see what would happen. To her surprise, she discovered that Ed had extensive knowledge of the golf swing and had worked with a number of outstanding players—men and women, amateurs and professionals. After one session on the practice range, Betsy concluded that Donna had been right on the mark.

"Ed gave me direction," Betsy says. "I made a few adjustments, but Ed gave me confidence in my swing. I had the drive and basic fundamentals. I just needed the right direction."

A year later Betsy won a tournament in Japan.

And finally, during her seventh year as a pro, she won on the LPGA Tour in the United States.

From that point on there was no stopping Betsy King.

In 1984 she won three times, becoming the leading money winner and the women's Rolex Player of the Year. Over the next three years she notched her name on the winner's trophy at fourteen venues, including her first major championship at the Dinah Shore in Palm Springs.

But her dream of winning the U.S. Women's Open still eluded her.

In 1989, her thirteenth year on the LPGA Tour, the United States Golf Association chose the Indianwood Golf and Country Club in Lake Orion, Michigan, to decide the number one player of women's golf. Betsy was playing some of the best golf of her career, having won four times during the first six months of the year. The momentum continued. She cut ten strokes off par, shooting 278 over four rounds to fulfill her childhood dream of winning the Open.

That year she garnered a total of six championships, broke the all-time money-winning record for a single year, and won her second Rolex Player of the Year honors.

But her best golf was still ahead.

At an age when many professional golfers are winding down their careers, Betsy won five more tournaments, repeated as the U.S. Open champion, became the first player to amass $3 million in winnings, and led the U.S. Solheim Cup team to victory.

In 1992 she would become the first woman to shoot four rounds in the 60s in a major championship. Her near-perfect, record-shattering rounds of 68, 66, 67, 66 (267) at the LPGA Championship in Bethesda, Maryland, were later called "the best golf ever shot at an LPGA event" by LPGA Tour veteran Joanne Carner.

I chatted with Betsy in Bethesda immediately following her victory. She was in a warm, cheerful mood. The first question I asked was, "Was there a key to why you played so well?"

"Before I came to Bethesda," Betsy said, "I went to see my longtime teacher, Ed Oldfield. He didn't say much as we worked together on the practice tee. Mainly he reassured me that what I was working on was sound."

"Did you have any idea that you were going to play like you did?"

She shook her head, bouncing her blonde hair. "When I teed off on Thursday," she said, "I never dreamed what would happen over the next four days. I tried not to get too goal oriented—just play shot by shot and see what would happen. I got off to a good start and said to myself, *Well, it would be nice to keep doing that.*"

"You kept doing it."

Betsy smiled. "I told myself, just give your best. Shot by shot. Hole by hole. Day by day. Tournament by tournament."

"Even if you finish one-hundredth."

She looked me square in the eye and smiled again. "Or first."

After that win, the number of Betsy's firsts would be few; still, at the end of eighteen years on the LPGA Tour she'd won twenty-nine events.

One last dream was still unrealized: the Hall of Fame. To get into it, she needed thirty victories. One more.

My wife and I saw Betsy in the spring of 2004. We talked with her about the struggles she experienced seeking that one last win. She told us: "I remember thinking that if I didn't win, I was a failure in other people's eyes. People kept asking me, 'What's wrong, Betsy?'"

"You didn't win for about two years, as I remember."

"Not until Atlantic City in 1995. I was tied for the lead going into the last round." Betsy paused. Her eyes sparkled. She grinned as if she had a secret to tell.

"Ruth Harrison and her husband, the tournament directors, were standing on the first tee when I drop-kicked my drive—hit it maybe five yards. It was probably the worst drive I've ever hit as a professional." Betsy laughed. "I've never been so embarrassed in all my life."

"Yet you won the tournament."

"After my drive, I hit a five wood for my second, an eight iron on the green, and holed a forty footer for par." She laughed again. "I ended up making birdies on the last two holes and won by two."

Betsy went on to win four more tournaments, her last coming in 2001. Her career earnings put her eighth on the all-time list. She was named captain of the 2007 U.S. Solheim Cup team.

Betsy's story about learning from Ed Oldfield reminded me of an experience I had when I was playing the PGA Tour. I was walking onto the practice tee at Firestone Country Club in Akron, Ohio. Gary Player, who would go on to win nine majors, was the first person I came to. He motioned me to come closer and asked for my advice about his golf swing.

"Watch me hit a few, laddie," he said in his warm South African accent. I was pleased with my counsel and couldn't help but think that I'd given a golf lesson to one of the greatest players in the game. My chest swelled.

The next day when I came back to the range, Gary was grinding away again. But this time he was getting a lesson from one of the caddies. My puffed-up ego blew away like a wild-flying balloon that had just popped.

I've had the pleasure of getting to know Gary quite well over the years. One thing I've observed about him is that he is always picking brains. He said he sorts a lot of information, but he always wants to be learning.

Betsy, like Gary, was humble enough to seek the best golf doctor she could find. When she did, her career changed.

It's only when we admit what we don't know that we can find the help we need.

This humility is important in all of life. All of us can benefit from another person's insight and expertise. Proverbs 19:20 says, "Get all the advice and instruction you can, so you will be wise the rest of your life." Whether it's from a pastor, a counselor, a teacher, or a good friend, wise advice from another can give us a new perspective and renewed enthusiasm for our situation.

When you feel like you're stuck in the same place, or you aren't sure how to approach a problem, make the same choice as Betsy King. Listen to the advice of those you respect, seek out an expert, and ask for help.

Three things Betsy King did to become a champion

1. She didn't give up. When things weren't going her way—whether in one round or over several years of trying to win a tournament—she kept moving ahead.
2. She learned to focus on one shot at a time.

3. She listened to good advice. Even though she was a professional golfer, she agreed to work with a coach. She didn't let her pride get in the way of following his counsel.

DAILY AFFIRMATION

I choose to accept help from others.

3

THE TIGER WOODS STORY

Champions Choose to Risk Change

In June 2000, the world's top-ranked Tour professional had one goal when he arrived at Pebble Beach for the hundredth U.S. Open Championship: his name on the trophy, etched beside the greatest golfers in history.

Three years had passed since Tiger Woods had smashed the Masters scoring record at Augusta National and won his first major at age twenty-one.

His 1997 celebration at the Masters was short-lived. After the tournament he replayed the videotape. When he examined his swing, he realized that his upper body was out of sync with his lower body.

Butch Harmon, his coach at the time, was well aware of the problem, but how do you tell a man who has just broken the Masters scoring record that his swing is flawed?

Butch didn't have to.

Tiger saw it and knew that if he wanted to get better, he'd have to make a swing change. He'd have to take a risk. It meant he would get worse before he got better. It meant change. Work.

Tiger knew that to become more accurate with his drives and more consistent in his overall game, he needed to better synchronize his upper-body movement with his lower body. Too often on his downswing, his lower body would run ahead of his arms, causing the club to get trapped behind his body. From this position he was forced to flip his hands just prior to impact. My good friend Jim Flick, golf coach to Jack Nicklaus, calls this problem "playing catch-up." With Tiger's 1997 swing, his timing had to be perfect. At the Masters that year, it was. But he knew that he couldn't count on perfection. He needed a swing that would work even when he was a little off.

Three years passed. During the remainder of 1997 on through early 2000, Tiger trained his body to do what it had never done before and did not do naturally.

Out of the next twelve major championships he competed in, Tiger lost eleven.

The press and fellow pros had predicted that Tiger Woods would become the Michael Jordan of golf. He'd been compared to the all-time greats: Bobby Jones, Ben Hogan, and Jack Nicklaus.

By June 2000, Tiger had played five years on the PGA Tour and hadn't won a single time on a tight-driving course such as the U.S. and British Open venues. He'd been successful on wide-open courses, but not the more demanding ones. Some of the astute media people were asking if Tiger *could* win.

One day in spring 2000, Tiger was practicing on the range of Isleworth Country Club in Orlando, Florida. He was hitting full eight-iron shots.

Suddenly, like Rannulph Junuh, the hero of *The Legend of Bagger Vance*, he felt an electrifying sensation shoot through his arms, chest, and lower body. He grabbed his cell phone and called his coach. "Butch," Tiger exclaimed, "I've got it!"

Tiger Woods felt ready to put his new swing to the ultimate test: the U.S. Open at Pebble Beach.

By the time Tiger arrived on the Monterey Peninsula, he was playing the best golf of his life. Mark O'Meara, one of Tiger's closest friends on Tour and winner of the Masters and British Open in 1998, played three practice rounds with him. He later told NBC commentator Johnny Miller, "I've played the Tour twenty years. Tiger's the best player I've ever seen. The guy has everything. He drives it longer and straighter than anyone in history. He can hit it high or low. He can hit cuts and draws. He has more imagination around the greens than almost anyone. And his putting is great right now. How can he lose?"

On the first day of the one-hundredth U.S. Open, Johnny Miller forecasted that Tiger would win.

Still, Tiger had never mastered the narrow fairways and severe roughs of the U.S. Open. And earlier that year at the Masters, his game had fallen apart on Augusta National's back nine. When he had double-bogeyed the tenth and triple-bogeyed the twelfth, Vijay Singh had captured the title, defeating Tiger by eight shots.

The sky was brilliant orange that Wednesday as the sun dipped into the ocean at Stillwater Cove.

Tiger Woods left the course after a long session on the putting green.

He was ready for Pebble Beach and the one-hundredth U.S. Open. But was his new swing?

Up close, Tiger Woods seems taller than six-one.

Often Tiger is compared with basketball's great star Michael Jordan. Both superathletes have a towering aura that lifts them above the ordinary.

At the Skins Game in Palm Springs a few years ago, I was watching as Tom Lehman, Mark O'Meara, and Tiger were about to tee off on the ninth hole. That particular day Lehman was giving Tiger a shellacking. I overheard Tiger needling him.

"Tom, you've got to start giving us shots," he said. *Tiger Woods needing strokes? What a joke,* I thought.

Even on that particular day, when Tiger wasn't winning, I felt a sense of awe being near him. I recalled a similar situation when I was twenty years old and playing in my first U.S. Open at Inverness Country Club in Toledo. On the fourth hole my threesome played, the group that was playing behind us caught up to us. In that pairing was one of the most talented players ever to play golf, Sam Snead. Just as I was about to drive, he stepped on the tee and stood about ten feet from me. His presence made me so nervous that I became disoriented. I couldn't remember anything I was supposed to do to execute the shot. I had the same nervous, awestruck feeling a few years later when I had the opportunity to give President Lyndon Johnson some putting tips on the White House green.

Tiger always dresses immaculately. Every shirt and pair of trousers is pressed and wrinkle free. His posture is like a brick wall. He strides between holes and down the fairway like a U.S. Marine general. He's been called the first Green Beret Tour professional. He doesn't meander, even when signing autographs. He's always moving.

I've been around the PGA Tour for more than forty years. I've had the privilege to play in the same tournaments as Ben Hogan, Byron Nelson, Tommy Bolt, Sam Snead, and Jimmy Demaret. Then later with Arnold Palmer, Gary Player, Jack Nicklaus, Tom Watson, and Lee Trevino. But none of these men, with the exception of Hogan and Snead, had the aura that Tiger has.

★

White-capped waves were cascading in the ocean holes that Thursday when Tiger teed up his drive for the first hole at Pebble. The cypress seemed to be inhaling the fresh ocean breeze, and Tiger was competing against three indomitable foes.

First: Pebble itself. Jack Nicklaus said this is one of the best tests in golf and the course he would choose if he had one last round to play.

Second: The field. Vijay Singh, the reigning Masters champion; Phil Mickelson; and two-time Open champion Ernie Els were among the elite field that all had victory in mind.

Third: Himself. He knew what was needed: his new, improved swing, with flawless timing. He had to stick to the new way of playing, trusting that it would pay dividends even when it seemed difficult. He had to control himself no matter what happened, even if he had a bad hole. He had to make better shots, and putt and chip better. Better than any U.S. Open he'd ever played.

When he struck his first shot that morning he knew he'd prepared well. He'd been preparing for the Open for two decades, since his dad, Earl, an ex–Green Beret, first put a golf club in his hands.

Would his new swing hold up under the pressure of the ultimate test of tournament golf, the United States Open Championship?

The first round would be a barometer. Tiger wanted it to register high.

★

Tiger jumped out fast, carding a 65. He was exactly where he wanted to be. Leading.

Fog stopped the second round. Tiger didn't begin his first hole until 4:40 on Friday afternoon. By the time he reached the twelfth hole, it was nearly dark. He held a two-shot lead over European Ryder Cup player Miguel Angel Jimenez. Tiger elected to putt out on the par-three twelfth after play was halted. He did so to his advantage by making a long putt for birdie and increasing his lead to three.

His first major test came the next morning.

On the eighteenth hole he made a serious mistake. Selecting a driver, he pulled his shot. His ball struck the rocks and ricocheted into the salty waters of Stillwater Cove.

His upper and lower body had gotten out of sync.

Was this a repeat of Augusta? With a two-shot penalty, his lead had dwindled to one over Jimenez.

Tiger, at twenty-five, was a veteran. He'd played in a dozen USGA Championships as a junior golfer, amateur, and pro. But another bad shot, another ball in the water, and his dream of the crown might easily vanish.

"Trouble, like bananas, comes in bunches," former U.S. Open champion Orville Moody once told me. "You just try not to let one bad shot make you make another bad shot."

Tiger had been playing near-perfect golf. Sixty-five the first round. All he needed was a par on the eighteenth for 68 in this second round. Out of nowhere, he had hooked his drive into the Pacific Ocean. He knew he'd made an irreversible error. He was fuming.

The test: Would he allow one bad shot to make him make another?

He stepped back before hitting his next shot. Regrouping. Calming himself. Gearing his mind to make the best swing he could.

His drive flew three hundred yards into the fairway. Safe. He fired his ball onto the green and two-putted for the 69.

Tiger had bounced back.

Later that day he would face another defining moment.

Blustering, thirty-mile-per-hour winds had blown the fog away, but when Tiger teed off late, 3:30 p.m. on Saturday afternoon for his third round, conditions had worsened. Phil Mickelson, who went on to win the 2004 and 2006 Masters and 2005 PGA Championship, described the challenge: "The greens are so small, yet so hard, that with anything over a six or seven iron you just can't hold the green."

Tiger got off to an uneventful start with pars on the first two holes. The pivotal moment of the one-hundredth U.S. Open Championship came at the third hole.

On one of the easiest holes at Pebble, Tiger pushed his second shot to the right. The ball headed toward the bunker. When it hit the ground it took a bad bounce and nestled so deep in the kikuyu grass that Tiger could barely see it. Having been where he was on many occasions, I sensed what he must have thought: *I didn't hit that bad of a shot. Now I'm in jail.*

Most pros carry a lob wedge, which is the scoop-shovel of the golf professional. Even in the deepest rough the lob wedge can extract the ball. But the kikuyu grass at Pebble is unlike any other grass in the world. At times, you feel like you're hitting through barbed wire. Or, should I say, trying to hit through it.

Tiger assessed the situation. The steep-faced bunker of white sand stood between his ball and the pin. The ball was buried six inches below the surface of the snarling grass. It was unlikely, even with his best effort, that he would be able to float the ball over the bunker. And if it buried in the sand, he might make a double or even triple bogey. He elected to advance the ball sideways, back to the fairway.

Taking a full swing, he tore into the wiry turf with enough power to move the ball one hundred yards.

But Pebble's rough won. Tiger couldn't get through. He didn't even complete his swing.

The ball moved only inches.

Tiger assessed the situation again. This time the ball was slightly more visible, making the shot not quite as difficult, though it was still buried in the kikuyu.

Another powerful swing.

The ball moved seven yards.

Tiger was still in the rough.

He shook his head and swung again.

Finally, he got on the green.

Two putts.

Triple bogey.

Tiger walked off the green and looked at Steve Williams, his caddy. His mouth opened, revealing his shining teeth. Then he did something very unusual. He laughed.

"Couple of bad breaks," Tiger said. "That's all."

Every player in the field was going to have a few. Tiger had them on one hole.

Tiger was faced with another choice. Would he allow one bad hole to ruin a great tournament?

He regathered himself, as he had on Friday, and parred the fourth and fifth holes. But on the uphill, par-five sixth, his second shot found the kikuyu again. This time it rested on the three-foot ledge above the bunker, some sixty yards from the hole. To execute the shot he straddled the ledge with one foot in and one out of the sand. He slashed the ball out of the kikuyu grass onto the green and holed his putt for a birdie.

He played flawlessly the next seven holes.

On the fourteenth hole, he was about to pull off one of his greatest feats of the tournament.

The fourteenth is a monstrous hole, measuring 573 yards in length. It's almost impossible to reach the green in two shots, except with a tail wind. A huge bunker protects three-fourths of the green's left side, leaving only a small alley for entrance to the green.

Most of the players lay up their second shot to one hundred yards. From there they are at optimum distance to spin the ball with their wedge or sand wedge and keep it from bouncing over the green, a common problem on this hole.

Tiger launched a drive 315 yards, so long that he positioned himself to reach the green with a two iron. The next shot was even more incredible. He attacked the garage-door-size opening to the green and forced the ball onto the putting surface, leaving several thousand spectators who had lined the fairway wide eyed, their jaws hanging. He two-putted for a birdie and went on to complete the round with a 71.

He'd been resilient again. He'd chosen to leave his disastrous triple bogey on the third behind him and move on, just as he had done the day before at the eighteenth hole when he drove in the water.

The following day, his final round, was a walk on the beach. Not a bogey on his card. Scoring 67, he had broken nearly every record in U.S. Open history, including the seemingly unbreakable one: Old Tom Morris's record, which had stood for 138 years. Old Tom had won the British Open by thirteen shots, the biggest margin of victory in any major. Tiger won by fifteen.

One sportswriter wrote, "Michael Jordan never did what Tiger Woods did. . . . Winning the U.S. Open by fifteen is tantamount to scoring 100 points in game seven of the NBA finals, a feat made startling not only by the magnitude of the performance, but the stage on which it transpired."

As the first year of the millennium unfolded, Tiger accomplished what many consider the greatest golf ever played in a year.

Three weeks after Pebble Beach he won the British Open, making him the youngest ever to win the career Grand Slam—U.S. Open, British Open, Masters, and PGA Championship. Only Ben Hogan, Gene Sarazen, Gary Player, and Jack Nicklaus had ever won all four majors.

Later in August he won his second PGA Championship, becoming the first pro since Ben Hogan to win three majors in one year.

By the end of 2000, he had broken twenty-seven records.

Then in April 2001, he won the Masters, making him the only person who had ever held the titles of four major championships of golf simultaneously.

But in 2003, Tiger's game took a step backward. The following year, Vijay Singh knocked him out of his number-one ranking. Tiger said he felt "stuck" both with his swing and his coach, who was a good friend.

To get "unstuck," Tiger made a dramatic choice: He found a new golf doctor, one he believed could help him improve. It took another year, but improve he did. He regained the number one spot in 2005, and in 2006 he shot four consecutive 66s to win the Buick Open, followed by two major championships and a strong run of U.S. Tour wins.

It's hard to let go of something good.

Some of us—like Paul's clients Cynthia and Rachel, whom you'll read about later—are in the midst of extremely difficult circumstances where nothing in life seems right. Others of us may be fairly comfortable where we are. Our lives are moving along, we're holding to the status quo, we're doing okay. That's where Tiger Woods was when he decided to risk his success up to that point for something better. He let go of something good to reach something great.

The Gospel of Luke tells a story about seeking the greatest goal. Jesus was visiting the home of a woman named Martha. As she busily prepared a meal for her guests, her sister Mary sat near Jesus, listening carefully to his teaching. Finally Martha had had enough and asked Jesus to tell Mary to help her with the food. Jesus' response surprised her: "My dear Martha, you are worried and upset over all these details! There is only one thing worth being concerned about. Mary has discovered it, and it will not be taken away from her."[1]

What are the worthwhile things in our lives? Tiger Woods could have expended a lot of energy trying to win tournaments with his old swing, but that wouldn't have helped him reach his goal. Similarly, we can expend a lot of energy with small details in life and never remember our bigger goals. Tiger's spiritual beliefs are unclear; he's never spoken publicly on the subject. Nevertheless, we are in agreement with him that we need goals and must be willing to risk a change when necessary.

When we set a goal and take a step toward attaining it, we move toward the important things in life. Our job is to stop being satisfied with the status quo and set our goals high.

We believe God has great plans for each of us. But to find and reach them, we must be willing to risk change.

Three things Tiger Woods did to become a champion
1. He set a goal—to hone his gifts to the best of his ability—and he made a plan to reach it.
2. He risked change. He was willing to give up something good to reach something great, even though it would require a lot of work. He knew that choosing to risk change was worth the effort.
3. When he made mistakes, he moved on. He didn't get

caught up second-guessing himself or being angry at what had happened. Instead, he accepted it and moved forward.

DAILY AFFIRMATION

I choose to risk change and take one step toward attaining the most important thing in my life.

4

THE CYNTHIA ROWLAND STORY

Champions Choose to Get Up and Move On

Cynthia had boxed herself in to an inescapable situation, and she knew it. Since winning a national beauty contest and a college scholarship, she'd lived a secret life.

All during college and her early career as a television journalist, not even her close college friends, her parents, or her colleagues knew anything of her secret life. To them Cynthia was a star. Beautiful. Congenial. Capable.

That morning, no one knew she planned to call Bill Williams, her neighbor, and ask him if she could borrow a gun—on the pretense that she didn't feel safe—and then fire it into her temple. No one knew how deeply she hated herself or how she thought about herself—as a fat slob with no self-control who deserved to be dead.

She'd never told her parents or friends that she hadn't had a natural bowel movement in eight years.

No one knew how many times she'd secretly consumed in one sitting a dozen candy bars, a couple of pizzas, and two dozen donuts—and minutes later vomited them up. Or that she'd been bingeing and purging an average of four times a week for the past five years. No one knew that she'd popped sixty laxatives the day before.

No one understood her intense loneliness. No one knew how hard she'd tried but never felt she deserved to be loved by her parents and others. Not even her husband, who'd left her after four months of marriage.

No one knew she felt as if a monster lived within her.

She was Pastor Bob Rowland's daughter; she was supposed to be able to work out her problems. But she had failed and failed and failed.

Like the French existentialist, Jean-Paul Sartre, she believed there was "no exit" from her painful existence.

Except one.

She picked up the phone and dialed her neighbor. Neither Bill nor his wife, Beverly, was home.

Panicky, she ran to the grocery store. Another dozen donuts, a dozen candy bars, some yogurt, and a gallon of ice cream. And a hundred pink pills. She couldn't stop.

"I felt like a gremlin within me had taken control," she said. She quickly sped back to her home and locked the door. Then, strangely, a desire to resist overcame her. She had persisted for nearly an hour when the phone rang.

Joan Riker, a friend from her church, was calling. "Someone spoke at church today that I think you should meet," Joan said. "Her name is Jan Stevens."

Joan's call sparked a glimmer of hope within Cynthia. She called Jan Stevens immediately.

"Jan, you don't know me. Our mutual friend, Joan Riker, suggested I call you. My name is Cynthia Rowland."

"Cynthia Rowland, the news reporter?" Jan said. "I've seen you on television."

"I've got a serious eating problem," Cynthia said. "So bad I want to kill myself. I was planning to do it a few minutes ago when Joan called. She thought you might be able to help me."

"Please listen to me, Cynthia," Jan said. Her voice was clear and pronounced. "I know the agony you're going through. I've been right where you are now. But believe me, there is hope!"

She told Cynthia about the Meier Clinic in Dallas. Soon afterward, Cynthia walked into my office.

I had seen her before on television, when she was a news commentator. She was stunning—and a perfect weight in spite of having eaten 20,000 calories per day for a very long time. She admitted that she would take a short break between her television tapings, sneak off to a private spot where there was a candy machine, and put in a roll of quarters, eating dozens of candy bars before rushing to the nearby bathroom and forcing herself to vomit them back up. She would then brush her teeth quickly before returning to the set. But years of this results in a feeling of hopeless depression, suicidal ideation, a risk of death from lack of electrolytes (including sodium, potassium, and calcium, which are lost in the vomit), yellowing of the teeth, weakening of the heart, a fear of emotional intimacy, and a host of other problems—fortunately all solvable if caught in time.

Unlike some of our patients, Cynthia did not need to be convinced that she was bulimic, addicted both to food and to over-the-counter laxatives. But we were disturbed when we learned that in the twelve years she'd been fighting her addiction, no one had told her she might have an eating disorder. When she confessed to her family doctor that she was eating 20,000 calories a day and compulsively vomiting them back up, he very naively told her to stop.

She could not stop.

The first step in any twelve-step group for overcoming addiction is to admit that by yourself, you can't stop. But with the help of God and through confession to others, you can. The apostle James said that confessing our faults and struggles to each other will result in our healing.[2] At the Meier Clinic Day Programs, we put that into practice, with tears of confession, compassion, forgiveness, rage, shame, codependency, and fears poured out daily. It was Jesus who so wisely said that those of us who mourn and grieve and cry will be truly blessed,[3] because mourning ultimately brings comfort.

When Cynthia arrived at the clinic, the first thing I did was give her a thorough physical examination. Her electrolyte level was so low that she was fortunate her heart hadn't stopped beating.

We assigned Mike Moore to be Cynthia's therapist. In the first three weeks, Mike began to unravel Cynthia's life, seeking to find some root causes of her eating problem. Cynthia worked hard at every assignment that Mike gave her, actively participating in our ninety-minute group sessions. But nothing unusual surfaced.

Then one day Carrie, one of the young women in the group, talked about a recurring dream where she struggled to breathe as she was being attacked by a stranger and raped. She felt like she was going to die.

Mike, skilled in dream therapy, probed deeper and discovered that when Carrie was four years old she'd had a severe asthma problem. One night her parents, attempting to relieve her, had filled the bathtub with steaming water. Then they'd forced her to lean over the edge of the tub. Carrie had screamed in fear that she might fall into the boiling water.

As Carrie wept, Cynthia's chest deflated in anguish and she, too, began to cry uncontrollably.

Mike turned to her. "What are you thinking, Cynthia?"

"About when I was in the hospital," Cynthia faltered. "I was four years old then, too. One morning three big men and three big women came into my room."

"What happened?" Mike asked.

"It was a horror. The reason I was in the hospital is that I was burned. Unbelievably so. My brother had playfully bounced me off my bed into a boiling vaporizer that had set my lower body on fire.

"The six people who came into my room were orderlies and nurses. They began to spread my legs apart and remove the bandages," she said. "I cried out to them, 'Please, please, I'll be good.' But they kept on. They touched me where I'd never been touched. 'Please, stop. I'll be a good girl. Please go away.'

"One of the nurses yelled back, 'Well, then, go back to sleep and shut up.'

"I screamed for Daddy and Mommy, but they were not there." Cynthia wiped the tears streaming down her cheeks. "I thought maybe I'd done something bad and they didn't love me. I felt like I'd been abandoned."

Something clicked for Cynthia as she relived the painful day of her burning and feelings of abandonment at the hospital. "It wasn't until I heard Carrie's story and relived those anguishing days," Cynthia said, "that I realized it was there at the hospital when I decided that I was damaged freight."

Cynthia now realized why she had always felt she was ugly, but she still didn't know the way out. With our entire team of a therapist, a group therapist, a nurse, doctors, and other loving patients probing into deep unconscious conflicts,

Cynthia unraveled a number of painful fears and experiences she had buried deeply.

It took a couple of months of daily therapy for Cynthia to be rid of her bingeing and vomiting habit for good. Now she needed to write a new script for her new life, which would include ridding herself of subscripts like, "I'm ugly," "I'm just a piece of junk," "I need to be perfect," and "I can never do enough."

Her progress was steady until a short time later when her parents came to the clinic.

Cynthia had tried to please her parents since her teenage years—to her physical detriment. At twenty-eight she still believed she would be more acceptable to her parents if she was thin. But by the time her parents arrived, Cynthia's life script had changed. She no longer believed she was damaged freight.

"I had a death wish," she told her parents shortly after they arrived. "I attempted to take my life."

"Why didn't you tell us?" her mother asked.

"Because you wouldn't have believed me," Cynthia said. "A year ago I told you I was taking sixty pills a day and you said, 'You don't do that.'"

Cynthia actually had wonderful parents, but even wonderful parents make mistakes, as every human does.

"I guess I was in denial that my perfect daughter was sick," her father said.

"I hate being your perfect daughter," Cynthia said. "The pressure's unbearable. I just want you to love me as I am."

At Mike's urging, Cynthia told her parents about being in the hospital, and how the nurses and doctors' treatment made her feel as if she were damaged freight. She concluded, "All my life I've worried about my scars from the burns." Suddenly the tone of Cynthia's voice cleared and the color of her face changed; her cheeks were pink with anger. Her tears stopped. "You said I might have to have plastic surgery, and I might not get married because the scars on my thighs would affect the man I marry. Messages like that always told me, 'You're not good enough.'"

Her parents shook their heads in shock. "We didn't know any of this. We're so sorry. We were concerned about your burns, but we never, ever intended to make you feel you were not good enough. We were only worried that your scars might make you feel inferior. We didn't know any better. Please forgive us."

Later that day, Cynthia did forgive her parents.

When her parents left Dallas, Cynthia's confidence surged. But the very next day the feelings of hopelessness reappeared. She felt big and ugly.

By 11:00 that night, the monster had taken over once again. At a moment when no one was watching, she consumed twelve palm-size cookies that she had stolen from a depressed male patient.

Suddenly, she panicked. *What have I done?* she thought. The next morning she told Mike what had happened. He explained to her it was part of a "setup" she'd accustomed herself to.

"Whenever I get close to being loved or am having a good time," Cynthia said to Mike, "I'll tell myself, 'I'm scarred, damaged freight. I don't deserve to be loved. I don't deserve to have a good time.'"

Mike was gentle and explained to Cynthia that she was beginning to understand herself. Regression was part of her growth. When she left the clinic, she would meet times of regression, and she could not let an occasional setback defeat her. Later I reminded her that wise King Solomon, three thousand years ago, wrote in the book of Proverbs that a person who fails seven times but keeps trying is *godly*.[4] Not a failure, but a normal human being who is godly enough to keep learning from the failures.

After her treatment, when Cynthia got an occasional urge to purge, she realized that her brain was trying to distract her from some truth that she was afraid of. So instead of bingeing and vomiting, she prayed that God would give her insight into what emotion she might be hiding from herself. When she learned her own unique emotional triggers, she could go to insight much more quickly and avoid even the temptation to binge and purge. When the truth sets you free, you become free indeed.

Now she faced a new choice. Would she continue to reject the life script that she was damaged freight? And would she choose to believe that, even with her scars, she was deserving of love and enjoyment in life?

Cynthia's life was so transformed during her three-month stay that when she left us, she began to speak about her experience publicly. Soon after, she formed an organization called Hope for the Hungry Heart, which is dedicated to helping others who suffer from eating disorders. It soon grew into a national movement. From Cynthia's recovery came the recovery of thousands of other bulimics.

Cynthia is a champion in the majors of life. I believe she became one because she made an important choice. She was resilient. She was willing to get up one more time. Get one more opinion. And try again.

It was the men's gymnastics all-around competition at the 2004 Summer Olympics in Athens, Greece. The world's top gymnast, Paul Hamm, led all his competitors after the first three rotations in the floor exercise, pommel horse, and rings. He had won the all-around gold at the previous world championships, and expectations here were high.

In the vault, usually a strong event for him, disaster struck. He completed one and a half somersaults, but he landed off balance and fell off the mat. He was obviously embarrassed when a judge had to help him up.

All his life he had trained for this moment. In seconds he'd thrown it all away.

As he sat down a few moments later, the electronic scoring board rattled off his score. He'd dropped to twelfth. The world champion looked to be out of contention not just for the gold medal, but for any medal.

Most people would have responded to this letdown by feeling depressed. Paul Hamm rejected this notion. Instead, he reminded himself of his coach's words: "It's not over until the meet is over."

He chose to accept his mistake—not dwell on it—and do his best on his last two rotations. "After that mistake I thought there was no chance to win the gold medal," Paul said later, "but I thought I could win the silver, maybe bronze."

He bounced back on the parallel bars and high bar with the two greatest routines of his life to win the gold medal by 0.012 points.

In the few seconds before he put his hands around the high bar for his final performance, he'd written a new script for his life. He left his failure behind and put forth the greatest effort he was capable of.[5]

His teammate Brett McClure said that Paul was frustrated after his fall. "But the great ones take that frustration and direct it toward an event and put up a huge number."

Like Paul and Cynthia, all of us fall. We make mistakes that seem disastrous. It's natural to dwell on our mistakes, but if we do it obsessively, depression can result.

There's another option: Choose to accept the disaster, get up again, and move on.

Cynthia Rowland and Paul Hamm experienced visible failures on a large scale. Millions of people were watching the Olympics on TV as Paul fell at the end of his vault. Cynthia was a well-known television journalist when she came to our clinic. Both could have let embarrassment at their problems immobilize them. But instead, they set aside worries about what other people would think. They set aside their own anxieties about their past failures. They determined to get up and try again.

Our failures may not be on as large a scale as Cynthia's or Paul's. But each one of us has failures. And if we're honest, most of us have *recurring* failures in the way we interact with people or the way we approach life. Whether it's anger, selfishness, anxiety, or impatience, every day we fall short of what we want for our lives. The Bible is clear that we also fall short of God's plan for our lives. "For everyone has sinned; we all fall short of God's glorious standard."[6]

But there is hope! God himself gives us grace when we fail. He forgives us when we do the wrong thing. The Bible even says, "He has removed our sins as far from us as the east is from the west."[7] God himself helps us write a new script for our life.

If he forgives us again and again, how can we not forgive ourselves? Resting in that incredible forgiveness, we are able to accept where we are, get up, and move forward, full of hope to try again.

Three things Cynthia Rowland did to become a champion

1. She sought help. At her lowest point, Cynthia admitted that she couldn't handle life herself. She took the advice of a friend and found therapists and doctors who could help her.

2. She forgave herself and others. Cynthia's recovery moved forward when she was honest with her parents and forgave them for ways they had hurt her. Forgiveness allows us to move past old problems and toward healing and wholeness.

3. She never gave up. When Cynthia slipped back into unhealthy patterns, she didn't throw in the towel. She accepted her mistakes, got up, and moved on. She believed that things could change, and by that positive attitude she wrote a new script for her life.

DAILY AFFIRMATION

I choose to accept my failures, get up, and move on.

5

THE LINDA ARMSTRONG KELLY STORY

Champions Choose to Find a Way

This story begins in a small town north of Dallas, Texas, called Plano. In 1971, the oil and gas industry was making Plano a boomtown. Linda was just sixteen, a junior in high school. It seemed like every family in town was getting rich except Linda's. Her parents were divorced. Her dad was a good man, a Vietnam veteran, but an alcoholic. She lived with her mom, who was trying to raise three children.

Linda had a boyfriend, a rugged young Texan. She thought she was in love, and she gave herself to him. But the unexpected and unwanted happened: Linda got pregnant. Neither of them was ready for the responsibility of a child. Though her boyfriend wanted Linda, he didn't want the baby.

She did.

She knew life would be easier if she aborted the baby. She could marry, her husband could work, and she could finish school. If she went ahead and birthed a child, she wasn't sure her boyfriend would stick with her.

She hid her pregnancy as long as she could to avoid pressure from anyone who might tell her to have an abortion. When her stomach enlarged, she started wearing baby-doll shirts.

But her secret soon became impossible to keep. When she told her mother that she was pregnant, her mother said she had two choices: abort the baby, or get out of the house.

Linda chose to have the baby and accept the consequences. She married her boyfriend, and a short time later, she gave birth to a little boy. Soon after, the marriage broke up. Suddenly, Linda was alone. She had no husband and no high school diploma, and she felt unprepared to sustain herself in the world.

She was not going to quit. She remembered something her grandmother had said: *Make every obstacle an opportunity.*

Linda believed she had made one good choice: to have the baby. Now she made a second choice: to find a way to turn her obstacles into opportunities. She decided to stay in school and let nothing deter her from getting her diploma. She knew she would never get a decent job and have the money she needed to support her baby boy without a high school education.

Linda searched for a good part-time job that would pay enough for an apartment and basic necessities for herself and the baby.

She struck out. There was no such job.

She refused to wallow in self-pity. She was determined to find the way.

She took two jobs, one in a Kroger grocery store and another in a Kentucky Fried Chicken restaurant. She worked hard, but even with two jobs she was only pulling down four hundred dollars per month. Still, she found a tiny apartment for two hundred dollars, and by disciplined spending she was able to finish school.

Time passed. Linda found a better job with the post office and later with Ericsson, a telecommunications company. She made sure her little boy had all he needed. Eventually she met another man and married again.

The little boy didn't like his stepdad and didn't know why.

Things were tough for Linda's young son. She didn't have the money to dress him like the other rich kids. One day a girl laughed at him because he was wearing old clothes. This stabbed her little boy in the heart, and Linda felt the pain, too.

She watched as her son searched for acceptance. He tried to play football, then basketball, then baseball, but he failed repeatedly at anything to do with hand-and-eye coordination.

Finally, at age eleven, he tried swimming. He liked it, but he was so far behind the other children that the swimming coach said he would have to swim with the seven-year-olds.

He was humiliated, but still he liked swimming. Linda told him he could turn this obstacle into an opportunity.

He believed his mother and worked hard. It wasn't too long before he won his first meet. He won other meets.

Meanwhile Linda was saving every cent so she could buy him a special gift for his birthday—a Schwinn bike.

When she gave it to him, his eyes brightened. Immediately, he took off. The bike represented freedom. Speed. He loved to ride fast.

One day when he was a young teen, he saw an advertisement for a triathlon called IronKids. He knew he was pretty fast on the bike and a good swimmer, so he entered the race.

He found out he was fast enough as a runner, too, and he won the contest. He won other triathlons, even men's events.

As a teenager, Linda's son discovered a letter he wasn't supposed to find and learned that his stepdad had a relationship with another woman. He didn't tell his mother about the letter, but Linda found out on her own. Later she got a divorce.

Linda faced another choice. She had exercised poor judgment in choosing her marriage partners. But rather than focusing on the past, Linda chose to look for the diamond in the Dumpster. She would turn this obstacle, too, into an opportunity, and continue to support her son.

As Linda's son, Lance, continued to improve as an athlete, someone told him he ought to enter a bike race. He did. He was even better on the bike alone than in the triathlons.

He finished high school and became a professional cyclist.

His career blossomed quickly in the next few years, until one day he got sick. Real sick. He hated hospitals, but something was wrong. After extensive testing, he met with his doctor, who had a sad look on his face. "You have cancer," his doctor said. "It's spreading through your body rapidly."

His doctor gave him less than a 5 percent chance of survival. He was only twenty-five years old.

It was July 14, 2003. My wife, Lorraine, a close friend, Jeremy Kelton, and I were in the French Alps, close to the Swiss border.

It had been seven years since Linda's son, Lance, found out he had cancer. He didn't die. In fact, he came back so gallantly that he became a cycling legend. He was here competing in the most famous bicycling event in the world—the Tour de France—championing the U.S. Postal Service team.

I knew practically nothing about professional cycling. I'm a golf professional.

I was curious why millions of spectators would line the sides of this two-thousand-mile, twenty-one-day race around the inner borders of France. I've been in stadiums for three of the last four Olympic Games and in other stadiums to watch American football. I've been at many U.S. Open and British Open golf tournaments, but none of these audiences compared to the Tour de France.

The Tour claimed the television audience would number close to 1.5 billion, which puts it with World Cup soccer and the Olympic Games as the largest television audience for a sporting event. But why would so many people watch a bicycle race? I planned to find out.

Les Gets is a little village in the French Alps only eight blocks in length. It's the last village before the riders descend into Morzine, a charming town surrounded by mountains, not far from the border of Switzerland.

We found what I thought was the last parking place in Les Gets and hurried back to the road where the riders would soon race by.

We stationed ourselves behind the waist-high portable fences, not far from a white line that crossed the road and marked the summit. More than five thousand gendarmes

(French police) would guard these aluminum barricades this year.

My heart was thumping as we waited for the cyclists, but my enthusiasm wore thin after standing behind the barricades for sixty minutes.

Finally the first racer came toward us. I stared through my camera, but he steamed by moving as fast as a car. I didn't click the camera because I couldn't see him. When I looked up, another rider flew by. I was looking for blue. U. S. Postal Service blue. I wondered where the current Tour champion, Lance Armstrong, was.

Just then a group of cyclists appeared, moving quickly toward me. The French call this main body of cyclists the peloton.

I saw some blue. My heart was thumping. We raced back to our car and followed the last cyclist down the windy mountain road into Morzine.

Later that night, to our delight, we ate at the same restaurant as the U.S. Postal Service team. We arrived early and were seated when the team—nine racers, two managers, four mechanics, eight others, and Jogi Mueller, the public relations director, came in and took their places around three tables.

Later I met with Pavel Padrnos from the Czech Republic. Pavel was one of the members of the U.S. team. Speaking in broken English, Pavel said to me, "My goal is to help my teammate, Lance Armstrong, succeed. When I'm out in front cutting the wind, I find joy knowing I'm helping a friend. Lance may become the second man in history to achieve five straight Tour de France yellow jerseys."

The yellow jersey, I learned, is the symbol of the overall champion. At the end of each day's stage, the yellow jersey is presented to the man who has the lowest total time.

"If Lance wins, that is good," he said, smiling at me like a seven-year-old. "If I win one stage, that is good, too."

I asked him what his most exciting moment of the Tour had been.

"The team time test," he said, smiling again. "We tried for three years to win it. Last year we were second. This year we won."

"And the most difficult moment?" I asked.

"Yet to come. Maybe tomorrow. The next three days are very, very, very hard. Alpe d'Huez will be the hardest climb." He leaned back and sighed.

The next day's trek would cover 131 miles, ending with 21 hairpin turns up the steep, eight-mile, 4.5-degree incline into the Alpe d'Huez village.

One sportswriter compared the endurance expended by cyclists in the Tour de France to that of a marathon runner competing in twenty-one consecutive marathons.

The Alpe d'Huez promised to be the marathon of all marathons.

"Lance is four minutes behind now," I said to Pavel. "Isn't that more than he wants to be?"

Pavel shook his head.

"Will he win?" I asked.

"He will win the Tour de France. Easily . . . no, not easily. He will win if he doesn't get sick or if something else doesn't happen."

Something had already happened. In one of the early stages of the race several of the cyclists piled up. Lance fell. Fortunately, he was not injured.

The next day, Lorraine, Jeremy, and I hiked all over Alpe d'Huez and made our way through the crowded streets to the finish line. We wanted a good vantage point to see if Lance would win the stage.

Even though we arrived five hours early, both sides of the road were already lined with people. Our standing place was an arm's-length opening on the green barricade fence about ten meters from the small stage where the winners of the day would receive their jerseys.

We passed the next five hours watching the race on a large outdoor television screen.

At about four o'clock Robert Farese, an American doctor who spoke French and could understand the television commentary, told me the American team was staging a comeback.

"Lance will have a big challenge to get the yellow jersey," Robert said. "He's more than two minutes behind right now."

An hour later, I was standing with Lorraine, eagerly waiting to see the first rider. We hoped he would be wearing blue. To our disappointment, an orange-jersey racer appeared first. Everyone in the crowd cheered except Lorraine and me.

Lance would not win the stage.

Another racer approached, not sporting the blue Postal Service uniform either. It seemed certain that Lance had not made up the two minutes.

Then a third rider. Blue. It was Lance Armstrong. Maybe he had picked up the two minutes after all. He was only a second or two behind the second cyclist. The crowds, mostly French, were cheering as loudly for Lance as for the day's winner, which made us feel good.

Before all the other racers finished, the awards were presented. To my surprise, Lance appeared on the podium. An official clad him with the yellow jersey. Armstrong had taken over the lead, even though he did not win this stage of the Tour.

Would Pavel's prophecy come true? Would Lance Armstrong win his fifth Tour de France?

It was July 26, 2003. Lorraine and I were back in the States. This day, the last stop before Paris, would determine the winner of the one hundredth Tour de France.

Lance still wore the yellow jersey, but he was less than a minute ahead of his chief rival, former Tour champion Jan Ullrich from Germany. If Lance maintained his lead, he would be almost certain to win as the cyclists raced into Paris the next day.

Rain drenched the tiny, windy roads. All but Lance and Ullrich had dropped out for the day. Ullrich was racing boldly in the slick, dangerous conditions.

Lance followed, starting quickly. Two minutes passed. Ullrich had closed the gap. He was racing fearlessly. Suddenly, as he cut to the inside edge of a curve, his wheels slipped out from under him.

He was down, sliding across the pavement.

Just as suddenly as he fell, he was back on his feet and onto the bike.

Seconds later a telecaster said, "Armstrong has the news that Ullrich has fallen. He's slowing. He won't risk anything now. He knows the only way he can lose now is to fall."

Ullrich fought hard, but in the end he fell short of Armstrong by sixty-one seconds.

The two champions had battled village roads for 3,400 kilometers (just over 2,050 miles) over twenty straight days. Ullrich's trek took 83 hours, 42 minutes, and 13 seconds. Lance's journey took 83 hours, 41 minutes, and 12 seconds. One minute, one second separated the two champions. Lance's average speed was the fastest ever raced: 40.94 kilometers per hour.

Lance Armstrong, the son of his devoted mother, Linda Armstrong Kelly, had come back from cancer, two crashes, and being run off the road into a field and won his fifth consecutive Tour de France.

Lance went on to win the Tour de France two more times. When he retired in 2005, he had an incredible seven consecutive wins.

When he accepted his final yellow jersey in Paris, he was accompanied by his three children. And immediately below the podium was a petite blonde woman gazing up at her son.

Linda Armstrong Kelly. A woman as amazing as her son.

A few years before, Lance was competing in the Road World Championships Road Race in Oslo. He was alone. It was cold. He called his mother and asked her to come soon.

It was raining the morning of the 161-mile event. Linda sat on the metal bleachers, watching the race on a huge projection screen. The road was slick, and many riders fell. When Lance rounded a corner, his wheels flew out from under him.

"Lance, you're okay," Linda yelled. "Get up."

He got back onto his bike and rode on before falling a second time and getting up yet again. The race went on for agonizing hours in the cold rain. Suddenly, Linda saw his face on the screen and recognized the determined look in his eyes. *He's doing it!* she thought.

Lance stood up and pushed down on the pedals, pulling away from the peloton. He soared over a hill and down a long descent to win the race.

In her book, *No Mountain High Enough,* Linda describes meeting Lance after the race. "Lance held me in his arms, my feet barely skimming the ground, and we buried our faces in each other's shoulders and we cried.

"'*We did it! We did it!*' he said over and over. . . .

"It felt like a finish line of sorts, Lance said later, for the race we two had run together. Everything we had at that moment, we'd given to each other. It was the sum total of all those years of hardship and happiness and struggle and love."[8]

Linda Armstrong Kelly sacrificed and supported her son, but the Bible tells us that we have an even greater supporter. In Psalm 27:10, David writes, "Even if my father and mother abandon me, the LORD will hold me close," and in Romans 8:39, God promises that "Nothing in all creation will ever be able to separate us from the love of God that is revealed in Christ Jesus our Lord."

His mother's love, support, and example planted in Lance Armstrong the determination to find a way, the perseverance to work hard, and the confidence to win. God can give us all that and more.

He will help us find a way.

Three things Linda Armstrong Kelly did to become a champion

1. She accepted difficulties.
2. She was willing to work hard and sacrifice for her ultimate goal. Linda devoted much of her life to supporting her son and helping him reach his potential.
3. She turned obstacles into opportunities. When things didn't go her way, she looked for the "diamond in the Dumpster" and taught her son to do the same.

DAILY AFFIRMATION

I choose to turn my obstacles into opportunities.
I will find a way to reach my goal.

6

RACHEL'S STORY

Champions Choose to Face Their Problems Head-On

When Rachel (not her real name) was sixteen years old, her chief interest was band. She loved to play the clarinet. The summer after her junior year in high school, the band was traveling by bus to a neighboring town. The bus arrived fifteen minutes late, and Rachel forgot her clarinet as she hurried out. As soon as she entered the stadium, she realized she didn't have her instrument and found the band director, Mr. Johnson. "I'm sorry," she said. "I forgot my clarinet on the bus."

Scowling, he waved her toward the bus. "Get back there," he shouted. "You're holding up the entire band."

It was pitch-dark in the parking lot. Red, the bus driver, saw her running toward him and opened the door. "Hi, Red," she said, trying to be friendly. As soon as she stepped in, the door of the bus locked, loudly. Red, a hefty ex-Marine, glanced up at her. He looked strange.

"Can I help you?" he said, starting to get out of his seat. Rachel shook her head. The look on his face made her feel uneasy.

"No, I just forgot my clarinet."

As she hustled down the aisle, she heard Red's footsteps behind her. Just as Rachel reached up to get her clarinet from the shelf, Red's right hand caught hers. He pushed her back into the seat. "I've been waiting for this moment since I first met you six years ago," he said.

Fear-struck, Rachel gazed into his face. She froze.

"You scream and I'll hurt you," Red shouted like a drill sergeant, as he clawed his right hand into Rachel's left hip. He forced her back into the middle of the aisle and down on her knees. A sharp, stabbing pain shot up the left side of her body. She swallowed her scream, petrified.

I was the second person Rachel ever told that she had been raped that night. She told the band director, but he convinced her to keep quiet. Later he, too, raped her.

When she told me her full story she was thirty-six years old and married. But neither her mother nor her husband knew of this incident or of the incredible fact that she had been molested or raped thirty times by eleven men over a period of twenty-five years.

Rachel had been carrying this secret for two and a half decades.

After she told me this story, she asked me to read her journal, which vividly detailed her horrors.

Her first entry was when she was eleven years old and living in a hotel where her mother was the manager. The hotel was nicknamed the Grand Hotel, but the beaten-down building was anything but grand. "I never knew my father," Rachel wrote. "After Momma gave birth to their sixth child, he left us."

The Grand Hotel was sold to a local college. When the sale closed, some vagrants were living in several rooms in the basement. The college did not want bad publicity from evicting the poor, so they allowed the vagrants to stay as long as they paid a small monthly fee.

Rachel's mom told her to stay away from those "grubby men with the whiskers." Rachel minded her mother. She didn't like them anyway.

One day after school, when Rachel was eleven, her mother asked her to go get the laundry out of the drier, which was downstairs in the basement.

Rachel had never done this alone, and she smiled. She felt like she was "mom's big girl," a phrase her mother affectionately used at times.

She skipped down the stairs with her light blue laundry basket in her arms, eager to please her mom. At the bottom of the stairs she ran into Eldridge, one of the "whiskered men." His gray beard hung down to his chest. He wore dirty clothes. She skirted around him into the laundry room. As she was taking the clothes from the dryer, Eldridge crept into the room.

"I need your help, little girl," the dirty-looking man said. "Come with me." He reached out for Rachel's hand.

Rachel backed away; the man smelled like a toilet.

"Come on," he said. "It'll just take a moment."

Rachel didn't know what to do, and when he started toward her, her whole body froze. "Come on, little miss, come with me."

Frightened, Rachel followed the man out the door and down the hallway into his room.

Stacks of old newspapers, smelly clothes, used paper plates, and wadded-up McDonald's sacks littered his dark room. The stench was so repulsive that she pinched her nose.

She shivered.

"Sit here," he said, motioning to the edge of the bed. "Don't be afraid. I'm not going to hurt you." Eldridge Harper pulled up the only chair in the room so it was directly in front of Rachel, about three feet from the edge of the bed. He began to unbutton his shirt.

"Just be quiet. Do what I say, and nothing will happen to you." The repulsive man's voice was deep and strong. Rachel felt icy cold.

Then Eldridge Harper forced Rachel to undress as he did.

"When I got upstairs," Rachel said in her journal, "I told Momma, 'Something naughty happened.' Momma was so overwhelmed with all her problems that she blurted out, 'Oh brother. What now? What else can happen?'"

Rachel hung her head and ran to her room.

A few years later she wrote, "Even though Eldridge Harper didn't rape me, he cut a wound in me that has lasted a lifetime. I didn't tell Momma about the second time he abused me or any of the other twenty-eight times I was molested or raped. Each episode became more degrading. Each time the shame mounted. I have a hunch Momma knew, though. She just didn't know how to talk about it."

At a subsequent session, Rachel told me that she survived high school largely because of her love for music, and she made it through college obtaining a degree in music education. Following college she married Bill and found a job teaching music. "For the first time in my life I experienced some joy and hope," she said.

However, she told Bill nothing of her sordid past.

Not long after their honeymoon, horrid flashbacks struck. Once, while in Bill's arms, she vividly recalled one of the times she had been molested. She recoiled. "What's wrong? Have I hurt you?" Bill asked.

"No, it's nothing," Rachel said, ashamed to tell him what she had just relived in her mind.

"Bill told me, 'I love you,' many times. He endeavored to reassure me of his love, but I didn't believe him," Rachel said. "I couldn't believe anyone could love me. I felt like trash. No one loves trash."

The flashbacks of abuse and the sleepless nights continued. Rachel remained silent. Years passed. Flashbacks persisted. Rachel became depressed. She felt helpless, then hopeless. Her world had turned gray again.

Bill and Rachel tried medical help. But her counselor said it would take a lot of time and effort for her to get better. She was already feeling exhausted and depressed from the flashbacks and sleeplessness, and the thought of giving more effort was like adding more heat to a volcano that was ready to blow.

Finally, it blew.

Rachel was thirty-six at the time. The head of her music department told her that the former principal of the school, who had retired, had decided to come back and teach band. The department head was in a tight spot, but he had no choice but to make room for the former principal. There was not enough money in the budget or work for them both, so Rachel was fired.

Feeling all hope lost, she got into her black Ford Explorer and headed out of town. She began to drive faster and faster.

"It was the only way out," she said. "I'd thought about what I was going to do many times. I knew the road. That night I was going to end the agony. I made sure my seat belt was *not* secured. I pushed the Explorer harder to higher and higher speeds. It was dead silent on the lonely back road.

"I was driving over ninety miles an hour when I spotted the lateral concrete abutment that would, once and for all, end my despair.

"The abutment, sixteen feet wide and higher than our Explorer, served as a riverbed for flash floods. The road curved to the right and the concrete barricade sat, immovable, directly ahead of me. I couldn't make the turn. I never planned to.

"Instead, I jammed my foot on the gas pedal and plunged straight forward, aiming head-on toward the gray cement wall. But my steering wheel locked, for no reason, so the Explorer missed the wall. Instead, it nose-dived into a ditch.

"It sounded like a giant battering ram smashing into an old building. My body slammed into the crumbling steering wheel. But my head kept going, cracking into the windshield.

"I blacked out.

"I awoke twenty-five minutes later to some sounds from the CD player, which had kicked on from the impact of the crash. Dazed but alive, I listened to the lyrics:

Standing among the ruins of a dream . . .
Seeing no way out . . .

You can rise from the ashes again . . .
For what looked like your heart's demise
Has turned out to be a blessing in disguise

"I closed my eyes and lifted my hands to my face. My chest felt like it had caved in. Every part of my body was in pain. But there wasn't a scratch or a cut on my face, arms, or hands.

"I closed my eyes again and listened to the lyrics of the song again.

"'You can rise from the ashes again. . . .'

"I crawled out of the car and walked to the highway. A man in an old 1950 pickup stopped and took me back into town."

Not long thereafter, Rachel ended up in our Dallas clinic.

She looked downcast during our first meeting. When I looked her in the face, she'd glance away and lower her head, avoiding any direct eye contact. When I did see her face I observed that her eye movements were quick and jerky. I asked her a couple of nonthreatening questions about herself, her marriage, and her family. Immediately, she began to cry.

She said she felt hopeless.

The more we talked, the more compassion I felt for her. She seemed like a lovable, sweet woman, though she felt she was unlovable. I had a deep desire to help her.

During those first ten minutes together, I had a hunch I knew the root of her problem. I asked, "Have you ever been molested?"

Suddenly her head dropped. She began to cry and groan so deeply that she sounded like an injured animal. Tears began flowing down her cheeks. When she stopped, she began to tell me about the first time she was molested.

After our first session I made three brief notes about Rachel: (1) post-traumatic stress disorder; (2) severe depression and anxiety; (3) use Gestalt.

Rachel—like many of our patients—had come to our clinic as a last resort. Though she felt her situation was hopeless, I noted two outstanding qualities about her that we see in champions: first, a willingness to change; second, a willingness to work.

We began our therapy by having Rachel focus on her abusers. Since we had no way to bring her in touch with them directly, we did the next best thing. We asked her to imagine they had come to the clinic and she was facing them.

We began with Eldridge, the vagrant who molested her at age eleven.

People who are repeatedly abused tend to stuff their emotions. They feel it's safer not to share their anger. Yet this "stuffing" leads to harmful depression.

In our Gestalt therapy, we prepared Rachel for her encounter with Eldridge by encouraging her to tell him how she really felt. Then we sat a chair in front of her and asked her to imagine the whiskered molester sitting there. Rachel lowered the boom. She did so well that after the session Rachel looked me in the face and gave me a tiny grin.

I was encouraged. "Rachel, you will get well." I don't say that to every patient who comes and sees us. But I had a deep belief that Rachel would.

We continued to bring each of Rachel's abusers to that same chair. Rachel leveled with each of them, telling them in no uncertain words how they had harmed her.

In group therapy, she met with others who had been through similar battles. Sharing her story openly with the group seemed to take the power out of the secret she had kept for nearly three decades.

During the next three weeks, Rachel learned to forgive.

Her poor eye contact changed. Her downcast look disappeared, and she began to smile spontaneously. By the third week we were hearing her laugh regularly.

We taught her the power of internal dialogue, good and bad. We identified detrimental self-talk and taught her a new inner language. Rachel was a wonderful student and took every opportunity to work hard and improve.

When we brought her husband to the clinic, Rachel embraced a brand-new concept: She was lovable. As I'm writing this today I am pleased to say she is a happily married wife.

In the years that followed, she returned to college and achieved a master's degree in counseling. She became a leader in an international organization that helps both women and men who have been mistreated, abused, and forgotten in countries all around the globe.

Rachel is a champion. She knew she needed help, and she chose to seek another doctor. She was willing to get up and try again. She chose to face the reality of her past. She worked hard to acquire new skills, and because of that, she improved dramatically.

I'm not gifted athletically, but I still love sports and have close friends on both the Cowboys and Rangers pro teams in Dallas, where I live. I've had the joy of treating a number of pro athletes. I've seen many of them make the choices that help them "get better at life."

Athletes have a huge impact on our culture, but they also have problems and pressures. Many of them deal with loneliness, compulsions, and self-critical messages—maybe even more than the average person, because they're usually perfectionists.

I had one patient who ended up as a Hall of Fame football player. His father was so strict with him that he went all the way through his football career with a fear of failure. When he lined up on defense, at times his vision would be affected because of his fear of failure, his fear of displeasing his father. Eventually he chose to face this problem, find help, and make a plan to overcome it. He improved as a player because he was able to relax more. If you're uptight and constantly fear failure, you can't perform at your highest level.

Another client was a middle linebacker who played for a couple of different pro football teams. His dad beat him when he was a child. As a result, he hated his father and hated himself. He was a fierce competitor and a hard-hitting middle linebacker. He hit people to punish them. When he forgave his father and took steps to work through his father complex, he lost some of his hostility on the field. But in my mind he became more of a champion because he wasn't filled with all that hatred, sorrow, depression, and loneliness.

Rachel and these athletes have something in common: They faced their problems. Champions face a shortcoming head-on. Whether it is a result of their own actions or someone else's, they own it. They don't deny it. They want to leave the past and move forward.

I saw a patient today who was finally able to move beyond a tragedy in his past. He is a retired lieutenant colonel from the U.S. Army, and he has bipolar disorder. We'll call him John. Thirty years ago, his job was to shoot down Vietnamese airplanes. He was a true champion who put his life and his skills on the line daily for our country. John had fired 99,999 rounds of ammunition at airplanes without a single mistake, and some generals and other officers came to observe him fire his 100,000th round and give him an award.

As everyone watched, John's superior officer told him an enemy plane was coming. He gave the order to shoot it down. John did—but to everyone's horror, it turned out to be an American plane. Three crewmen were killed.

John felt guilty from then on, even though the incident was not his fault. The soldiers in the platoon with the three men who were killed felt sorry for John. They knew it had been an accident, and they knew how bad they would feel in his place. They found a large picture of the main pilot who had been killed, and all of them signed their names on the back with the message, "It was not your fault." Unfortunately, John was transferred and never received the photo.

The photo was returned to the commander of the pilot's platoon, who was a follower of Jesus. He kept it for the next thirty years at his home. He prayed regularly that someday God would help him find that colonel who shot down his pilot so he could be assured that he was not to blame.

Not long ago, the former commander went golfing at the course near his house. Typically, he shared a golf cart with a visitor who happened to be playing at the same time. On this day, he was matched with John.

After a little conversation, he discovered who John was. They both wept when they realized how God had brought them together.

After the round of golf was over, the former commander took John right over to his home and pulled out the photo with all the signatures. God had answered his prayer.

I would guess by the outcome that God considers both veterans to be champions. The commander was a champion because he prayed for John for thirty years, even when he didn't see any results—a choice that shows perseverance, which we'll read more about in the next chapter. And John was a champion because he dealt with his past and moved forward.

The Bible has a lot to say about facing the reality of our mistakes. The psalmist writes, "Finally, I confessed all my sins to you and stopped trying to hide my guilt. I said to myself, 'I will confess my rebellion to the LORD.' And you forgave me! All my guilt is gone."[9]

Confession and forgiveness lead to freedom. And even when a problem isn't the result of our own sin—as with Rachel, who was a victim of abuse—facing it and dealing with it, especially with God's help, still leads to freedom. Jesus said, "If the Son sets you free, you are truly free."[10] Once we have confronted the problem and made a plan to overcome it, we are able to move on. Our past no longer controls us.

The apostle Paul writes these encouraging words about moving away from the past: "Forgetting the past and looking forward to what lies ahead, I press on to reach the end of the race and receive the heavenly prize for which God, through Christ Jesus, is calling us."[11] That's a worthwhile goal for anyone.

Three things Rachel did to become a champion

1. She faced reality. She knew she had a problem, and she acknowledged it to herself and others.
2. She wanted to improve. Because of that, she was committed to taking action that would help her get better.
3. With the help of good counsel, she developed a daily improvement plan and worked hard at it. She didn't leave her progress to chance.

DAILY AFFIRMATION

> *I choose to face the reality of my problems*
> *and make a plan to improve.*

7

THE LEE JANZEN STORY

Champions Choose to Persevere

I was standing three feet from the moon-shaped putting green at Indian Wells Country Club, waiting to see Lee Janzen, one of only a few golf professionals who have won the U.S. Open twice. Jack Nicklaus, Hale Irwin, Lee Trevino, and Tiger Woods are others who belong to this exclusive club.

The sun had disappeared behind the reddish mountains that hug the southwest holes of the course.

There was a waist-high rope between me and the green, signaling fans that pros playing this week's Bob Hope Chrysler Classic in Palm Springs needed space to practice their putting.

Lee had asked me to meet him here for our interview, but he hadn't spotted me and I wasn't about to bother him.

Eventually Lee glanced my way. "Jim, come over here," he said, waving his putter and motioning me inside the ropes.

I was very curious what gave this man the capacity to win the U.S. Open, a feat that eluded Sam Snead and some of the greatest players in golf. At age thirty-nine, he wasn't overly impressive in size or demeanor. Six foot, light brown hair, a lean 175 pounds. Pretty ordinary. He could pass for a plumber or a car salesman.

He greeted me with a warm smile. "Let's talk here." He tucked his ball in his pocket and his putter under his right arm. "I've been thinking about your question," he said.

The week before, at the San Diego Open, I'd told Lee about the book Paul and I were writing. We hadn't had time for an interview there, so he suggested I meet him here to talk. I asked him to be thinking about what makes a champion.

"What makes the great champions is they find a way to win," Lee said.

"Can you expand on that? What do you mean by *find a way*?"

"It's painful to lose, so champions figure out a way to win."

Lee's second U.S. Open Championship, at San Francisco's Olympic Club in 1998, was a perfect example of finding a way to win—even when it seemed impossible. After three rounds, he was five shots behind the leader, Payne Stewart. In golf, making up that kind of deficit in one round is a

mountain to climb. But Lee never gave up, even in a seemingly impossible position.

"You found a way to win when you were five back going
into the last day at Olympic."

"Actually, I started out par, bogey, bogey, par, so I was
seven back going into the fifth hole."

"Payne Stewart was playing the best golf of his life. He
had led for most of the tournament. It looked like you had
no chance."

"I'd played well in two of my rounds and shot over par.
I knew Payne was playing well, but it was easy to shoot over
par on that course," Lee said.

On the fifth hole, the hardest driving hole on the course,
Lee drove into a cypress tree. "I was about 100 yards down
the fairway when the marshal came out, shouting, 'I've got
binoculars. I watched the ball go into the tree, and it didn't
come out.'"

"How long did you hunt for the ball?"

"I didn't. The evergreen trees at Olympic are so thick and
heavy I wasn't surprised the ball hadn't come out. I'd hit a ball
into one during a practice round and hadn't been able to find
it. I turned around and started walking back to the tee."

"Figuring you'd have a two-shot penalty and lose all
chances of winning the tournament."

"At that point, I wasn't thinking of winning. But I still
had a good chance of making the top sixteen, which would
put me in the Masters the following year."

Lee laughed.

His laugh puzzled me. A lost ball penalty would spell a certain double bogey. *My Japanese golf friends laugh at their golf maladies,* I thought, *but I've never heard of an Open champion laughing about a two-shot penalty.*

"I thought of the story I'd heard in the locker room," he said. "The superintendent cut down one of the cypress trees and out plopped five hundred balls!"

His face lit up like a ten-year-old boy who'd pulled off a prank. I laughed with him.

He told me what happened next. In that moment when everything seemed black, something unexpected had happened. Lee's ball had fallen out of the tree into the rough. His name was written on it, allowing his caddy to make a positive identification.

"What did your next shot look like?"

"I was still under the trees, and the ball was sitting down in heavy rough. It was a tough shot, sideways, only about twenty yards to the fairway, but I had to use enough loft to get the ball out of the rough and still stay under the branches. I think I used a seven iron. I hit a good shot. It landed out on the fairway but ran all the way across to the other side, just about in the rough."

"Then what happened?"

"I hit a six iron that clung to the pin, but it hit hard and bounced over the green. I was in the first cut of rough about twenty-five feet from the hole."

I knew this story, but it was exciting to hear Lee's first-hand account. His next shot was about to turn the tournament around. "What did you play your pitch shot with?"

"A lob wedge. I was downhill, and the green was very fast. All I wanted to do was get it onto the green and down to the hole."

"And it went in."

"Just like a putt."

"So you walked off the green saying to yourself, 'I just turned a six into a four.'"

"Yes, it could have been anything. If my ball had stayed in the tree there was no guarantee I was going to make six. I could have turned out the lights."

"Did you think you still had a fighting chance then?"

"My outlook changed for sure. I'd made a par on the hardest hole on the front nine for me."

We decided to call it a day and finish up by telephone. That was fine because the sky was now dark gray and I was cold. I also wanted to find out more about Lee.

Lee MacLeod Janzen grew up in Baltimore. His first love was baseball, not golf. Baltimore Orioles baseball. But that changed when, at age twelve, his father's company moved to Florida, where Lee started playing golf.

Lee played junior golf well enough to gain a golf scholarship to University of South Florida in Orlando, where his game began to blossom. In 1985 their team won the NCAA Division II championship. The following year Lee became the individual champion and their team repeated as national champion. Later that year he was awarded all-American honors.

He married Beverly, a college sweetheart.

His first try at qualifying for the PGA Tour came up short, but he gained a valuable year competing on the U.S. Golf Tour and became its leading money winner.

Lee won his PGA card in 1989 and joined the Tour full time in January 1990. His first win came at the Northern Telecom Open in Tucson, where he closed with a 65, one of his best rounds ever. He won his first U.S. Open at Baltusrol in 1993, tying Jack Nicklaus's scoring record for four rounds on that course. It was only the second time an Open winner had all four rounds in the 60s. Payne Stewart finished second, two strokes behind.

That fall Lee and Beverly's son, Connor MacLeod Janzen, was born.

We picked up on our conversation at the 1998 U.S. Open some time later.

"Lee, you had a lot of momentum after the good break of your ball falling from the tree and your chip in on the fifth hole," I said.

"On the next thirteen holes," he said, "I hit every fairway and green, except the tenth hole, and I was just on the fringe there. I got so much into each shot that I decided I wasn't going to look at the scoreboard. I didn't want the scoreboard to affect how I was playing in any way."

"You birdied seven, eleven, and thirteen, and you had no bogeys."

"I kind of lost track of what I was shooting on the seventeenth hole. I thought I was one under, not even for the tournament."

Seventeen at Olympic is a par-five hole nearly five hundred yards long that the USGA had converted into a par four. The fairway is nearly impossible to hit because of a severe left-to-right slope. A ball landing in the middle of the fairway ends up in the right rough. A slight pull of the tee shot lands the ball in the left rough where it stays. To hit the fairway, the ball must land close to the upper third of the fairway to stay in play. In other words, it is an extremely small target area.

All week the seventeenth hole had caused Lee trouble. In three rounds, he had a bogey and two double bogeys.

"So as you stood on the tee looking down the fairway, what were you thinking?"

"Well, I was only worried about my tee shot. I knew the double bogey on Saturday wasn't caused by my hitting bad shots. I just wanted my ball to land halfway between the middle of the fairway and the rough. And that's about where it landed. It still rolled down to the right side of the fairway."

"What happened?"

"The opening to the front of the green is very narrow, with bunkers on both the left and right guarding the green. I smoked my three iron. A slight fade. The ball hit the front right part of the green and rolled to the back, and I two-putted."

"You've said that was one of the greatest shots of your life. Did you look at the scoreboard on the eighteenth tee to see how you were doing?"

Lee smiled at me again, pausing before he spoke. "No, I knew from the crowds all day I was getting close. You feel their energy. But I never looked at the scoreboard until I putted out."

"You made a good, solid par to finish at 280. When you looked over at Olympic's huge white scoreboard, how did you stand?"

"I believe . . . I believe I was tied. When I putted out on eighteen, I glued my eyes to the scoreboard to see how Payne and everyone else was playing."

Lee's jovial spirit had disappeared. I could sense the tension he felt as he relived that moment.

"I took in the whole scoreboard. I had no idea what anyone was doing, but as the scorer posted Payne's score on the sixteenth, the crowd got noisy. His bogey put me one shot ahead, and I saw no one else close."

"You had to watch him play the last two holes?"

"I don't know if I was that nervous waiting to get married. I watched thirty minutes. It was excruciating."

Payne Stewart wasn't able to muster a par, birdie finish and Lee won the U.S. Open by one stroke.

"My wife, Beverly, was there in the locker room. I'd given it everything I had for the day. I was completely worn out. My emotions . . ."

"You broke up."

"Yes, we were both emotional. It's hard for me not to get choked up when I think about how I won. . . ."

"You persevered. You found a way when there seemed to be no way."

Lee grinned.

Champions never give up. Lee Janzen didn't give up when it seemed sure that he would lose the U.S. Open.

For one of Paul's clients, a teenager named Bruce, perseverance was the key to getting help for his erratic behavior. Paul tells how he and his parents never gave up as they searched for a solution.

In my profession, giving the proper diagnosis is critical. If someone is misdiagnosed, the problem will worsen.

I remember the day when seventeen-year-old Bruce came with his parents to our clinic. His arm was in a cast. When I spoke alone to his discouraged parents, they related that Bruce had been treated most of his life by child psychologists for obedience/defiance disorder. That is a sophisticated way of saying that Bruce was a bad boy, a rebel who defied authority and refused to obey.

"At times he's well behaved and sociable," his mother said. "Other times he's a loner and suspicious. He says he feels like his peers are out to get him. So he may pick fights and beat them up to scare them away. Sometimes he even puts his fists through the walls of our home. He's broken his hand twice now."

"Every few weeks Bruce erupts," his father said. "Many times he will remain in a state of rage for three straight days, breaking things, punching holes in walls, and performing other acts of violence. He can't sleep. He talks incessantly, spends money impulsively, and makes rash decisions. The slightest irritation will set him in a tirade."

Bruce had no dreams or hopes for the future. Later, when I interviewed him personally, he said he didn't think he would live to age thirty.

That day Bruce entered our day program at the clinic.

A few days later, during my second interview with him and his parents, I told them he had never been properly diagnosed. "He has what we call rapid-cycling schizo-affective bipolar disorder."

Bruce and his parents made a choice to accept my diagnosis and recommendation. One week later, after we placed him on Zyprexa, Neurontin, and Zoloft, he began to see improvement. Zyprexa, a dopamine medicine, removed his paranoid delusions. The Neurontin took away his mood swings. Zoloft, a serotonin medicine, prevented him from getting clinically depressed.

A few weeks into treatment, he had a vivid dream: He was wearing a heavy white cast on his right arm. His mother encouraged him to leave his cast on so he wouldn't hurt himself. At first he rebelled by taking it off, but then he smiled, feeling love for his mom, and put it back on.

The dream was simply showing him that his brain was adjusting and the medication was helping him. For the first time since he was about five years old, he was beginning to feel normal.

I have followed Bruce for half a dozen years now, and he has been faithful to take his medications and be productive, both at college and at his job. He now has a great relationship with family and friends. Bruce became one of the most enjoyable young men I have ever treated. But to stay well, he must have medication. Last I heard, Bruce was engaged to a sweet and loving young woman.

I consider Bruce and his parents champions. Through years of difficulties, they had tried many other approaches that failed because of incorrect diagnoses. But they hadn't given up. Like all champions, they persevered and chose to make a change—in this case, to find a new doctor. Had they been unwilling to get help, Bruce might still be living with a genetic biochemical abnormality in his brain. Had his parents not sought to get another opinion and had he not received the proper diagnosis and treatment, his brain chemicals would never have changed and he would still be flying into rages.

At times some of my clients wonder why they're even coming for counseling. I often hear them say, "Nothing's really going to help." They feel depressed and have little hope of getting better.

Often their problems are not that difficult to cure. It's not because I'm some superdoctor; it's more that our profession has come so far. Today, there are many ways to help people who want help. I'm completely convinced that many of the 20 million depressed people in the United States can overcome depression if they will make a few wise choices. Even if the depression is genetic, there are new medications available that can help people overcome problems that seem impossible.

If you catch some crickets, put them in a fishbowl with a little dirt on the bottom, and give them some good cricket food and a little water, they'll hop out of the bowl easily. If you put the same crickets in the same fishbowl, but put a lid on the top—with holes in it so they can still breathe—they'll try to jump out. But after they've hit the lid for a day or two, they'll quit. They'll give up because they believe they can't get out.

You can take the lid off, and they still won't jump out—because they don't think they can.

They can, but they don't think they can.

Most of us agonize to change some area of our lives, trying over and over. We don't know there's a way out of the fishbowl—but there is. Our first step out is a choice. We must ask ourselves, *Am I willing to try again after feeling like I've failed a thousand times? Am I willing to take a risk? Can I find a way when it seems there is no way?*

Lee Janzen found a way to win the U.S. Open when there seemed to be no way. Bruce and his parents never gave up looking for the right diagnosis and a cure.

Perseverance paid high dividends in their lives, and it can in our lives as well.

Pursuing a worthy goal is hard work. We may not see results immediately, and we are often tempted to give up and go back to what seems like the easier way. Champions choose to persevere. They keep hoping even when things seem hopeless. They find a way.

One of the most coveted prizes in golf is the green jacket given each year to the winner of the Masters. The green jacket of the Bible is a character trait: perseverance.

The author of the book of Hebrews writes, "Therefore, since we are surrounded by such a huge crowd of witnesses to the life of faith, let us strip off every weight that slows us down, especially the sin that so easily trips us up. And let us run with endurance the race God has set before us. We do this by keeping our eyes on Jesus, the champion who initiates and perfects our faith."[12]

What allows someone to "run with endurance"? Keeping a worthy goal in sight. For Lee, that was believing that he could win. For Bruce and his parents, it was believing that his life could improve. When we endure and believe, things change. The race may be hard now, but we know that God can transform our difficulties into a life beyond our wildest dreams.

When we keep our eyes on the goal, we're motivated and encouraged by what we see ahead. The process may be difficult, but the rewards will be great.

Three things Lee Janzen and Bruce did to become champions

1. They never gave up. Even when Lee was seven strokes behind the leader with only thirteen holes left to play, he persevered. He kept doing his best.
2. They believed that things could change. Bruce and his parents kept seeking the right diagnosis because they had faith that someone could help them.
3. They stayed focused on their goal. Bruce stayed on his medication because it allowed him to reach his goal of a normal life. Lee gave his all, shot by shot, and even stopped looking at the scoreboard—until he won.

DAILY AFFIRMATION

I choose to find a way and persevere until I reach my goal.

8

THE BYRON NELSON STORY

Champions Choose to Concentrate

In the office of my son, Peter, hangs a black-and-white framed photo of Byron Nelson.

The ten-by-fourteen-inch frame has two parts. At the top, it pictures Byron six feet off a green, sitting on the heels of his two-tone golf shoes. A white towel is hanging out of his back pocket. He is wearing a white beret-style cap, similar to one that Payne Stewart popularized during the peak of his career. In Byron's left hand he holds out a 1930s chrome-headed blade putter as he lines up his putt.

The bottom half of the frame contains a signed scorecard that notes all four rounds of Byron's 1937 Masters win.

In the right corner of the frame is a small photo of Peter, Byron, and me.

"Do you remember meeting Byron in the Troon hotel at the British Open, Dad?" Peter asked one day as we stood next to each other admiring the photo.

I had forgotten, but it came back quickly. It was about twenty years ago, and I was writing for *Links Letter*, a publication for golfers that I edited for eighteen years. I was hoping Byron would do an interview.

"We were in some private area where only the pros and their guests were permitted," Peter said. "Mr. Nelson had just finished giving a golf lesson and had been talking to Tom Watson. You asked him if we could talk."

Peter knew I had had the opportunity to play golf with Byron once when I was a student at the University of Houston and had a good relationship with him. "Right, I remember. Being a Texas gentleman, he obliged."

I thought back to my days on the golf team at the University of Houston in the late 1950s. I was in my room in Taub Hall when the phone rang. My coach, Dave Williams, told me, "You've been chosen for the Texas Cup Matches."

As one of twelve amateurs, I had been selected to play against the best of twelve Texas professionals. My opponent would be none other than Byron Nelson.

Just to caddy for "Lord Byron," as he was called by the media of his day, would have been privilege enough. But to compete against this man who had won eleven straight PGA Tour events and eighteen total events in one year was breath stopping.

I was awestruck most of the day of the match.

Watching this gentleman-statesman manage his game for eighteen holes remains one of my greatest experiences in competitive golf.

I've since learned one key to Byron's career. He won eight tournaments in 1944, but he wasn't satisfied. "I resolved to make 1945 my best year yet," Byron said at the start of the year. To do so, he said, he would "focus better."

Focus better he did. He got into a zone on March 11 and stayed there for three months, winning *every* tournament he played in. And seven more before the year ended.

Byron said that his two fundamental principles for playing competitive golf were composure and concentration. "Concentration," he said, "means paying attention so closely to what you're doing that outside distractions don't bother you. When you sense an interference, either from without or within, think instead about playing the shot at hand."

Byron was a man who lived life in the present. His huge success was in large part due to not thinking of the past or the future. Just the shot at hand.

This is true of all great champions. They don't play with cluttered brains.

They're focused.

One of my college roommates at the University of Houston and a three-time PGA Tour winner, Kermit Zarley, produced one of the most outstanding rounds of golf ever played in the final round of the NCAA championship at Duke University in 1962.

That year the individual NCAA championship was decided by match play. Kermit played against his teammate, Homero Blancas, in the thirty-six-hole final.

Homero played solid golf and shot two under for the day. But Kermit was near perfect, trouncing his teammate by a five-hole margin.

I had graduated by then. But later I asked Kermit what he shot.

"I don't know," he said. "I never kept track."

His words stopped me dead. I had played a few hot rounds in my career, but I always knew what I was shooting.

Kermit didn't know his score that day because it wasn't his major concern. He was intent upon executing just one shot at a time to the best of his ability.

Not long ago, Kermit told me he did remember his score for the first eighteen holes of play that day: seven under.

There's a story told about Arnold Palmer, and knowing PGA pros for over forty years as I have, I do not dispute it.

Arnold had a long putt on a particular hole in the thick of a PGA tournament. As he was lining up his putt, a dog broke through the gallery and raced across the green—right on the line where Arnold was intending to putt his ball.

Later in the pressroom, a writer asked Arnold, "Did the dog that ran across the green break your concentration?"

Arnold looked at the writer and with a blank face replied, "What dog?"

But my favorite story about concentration is about Larry Nelson, a longtime friend and winner of multiple PGA Tour events, including three major championships. Some time ago I talked to him about this subject in Oklahoma City. It was during the last event on the Champions Tour. We sat down together in the players' locker room at the Gaillardia Country Club.

It was Sunday morning and play had been delayed thirty minutes because of rain. It had been pouring all morning. I looked out the window, and the course was so soaked that puddles of water dotted the fairways.

Knowing we had only thirty minutes and might be interrupted, I asked Larry, "What's the difference between a good player—someone who has won a Tour event—and the truly great players?"

Larry is a soft-spoken, somewhat shy person. But he has a sharp, strong mind.

"Great players possess a focused awareness," he said.

He explained that great champions are aware of negative thoughts. "You may not be able to stop them from coming, but you can acknowledge them and then set them aside," he said.

"Can you give me an example of what you mean?"

"I've got a ten-year exemption," he said, gesturing with both hands. "And the thought that I'm exempt from qualifying for tournaments can keep me from staying focused."

"Like getting too comfortable or relaxing in your accomplishments?"

He nodded. "I think any thought that's about success, no matter what it might be, is a negative." I knew what he was saying. A professional golfer can't afford to get caught up in thinking about his or her success or what's going to happen in the tournament. Golfers can't worry about other players' scores and where they stand. They have to be committed, fully focused on the moment.

As I listened, my mind wandered back to one weekend when Larry had just begun to play the Tour. He hadn't won yet. But he'd caught a couple of good rounds and was leading the Jackie Gleason Inverarry Classic in Fort Lauderdale.

Lorraine and I flew down from our home in Washington DC to give Larry some support on Saturday and Sunday.

He played a solid round on Saturday and put himself in position to win against the biggest name in golf at that time—Jack Nicklaus.

We had dinner with Larry and his wife, Gayle, that evening. At one point, our conversation centered on Jack Nicklaus, the undisputed number-one player on the PGA Tour. The classic statement that night came from Larry: "Tomorrow will be the day," he said to Gayle with a sly look.

Gayle appeared puzzled.

"Tomorrow will be the day," he said again, "when we will know who is the greatest player in the world."

We laughed, but the next day, after nine holes, he was tied for the lead.

In those days there were no ropes between the ninth and tenth tees, so the players and crowd merged when the players walked between the front and back nine holes.

This is a great opportunity, I thought. *I'll catch him before he tees off and give him a word of encouragement.* I hurried up to Larry as he walked quickly toward the tee box of the tenth hole. "You can do it, Larry," I said. "You're playing well."

Larry totally ignored me. Never said a word. Never looked at me. Like a programmed robot, he marched toward the tenth tee. I wasn't sure if he had heard me, even though I was walking shoulder-to-shoulder with him.

I dropped back. "He's trying to stay focused," I mumbled to myself, trying not to feel spurned.

A few holes into the back nine, Larry grabbed the lead. At once I felt excited and queasy. I hoped I hadn't said the wrong thing to him. On the fifteenth hole I was walking with Gayle, and I told her what had happened.

"Oh, don't worry," Gayle said. "One time he didn't hear his dad, either. It was the same kind of situation."

Larry went on to win his first Tour championship, and during the span of his career he won more than thirty other tournaments worldwide.

As I look back on the forty-plus years that I've followed the PGA Tour, watching all the great players, I've noticed that they all possess, to some degree, this quality of concentration. It's the capacity to shut oneself off from the clamor and chatter in the world and stay 100 percent immersed in the business at hand.

Whatever our field, we can learn from the example of these champions Jim has described.

People mistakenly think concentration is hard. That's not necessarily so. It is a discipline, and like any habit, it takes time.

Developing a habit of concentration begins with a choice.

You can do it today. We all have things we need to concentrate on, whether it's studying, acquiring a new skill, finishing a project, raising children, or doing anything else. When we want badly enough to reach that goal, we make up our mind to stay focused on our one main desire. When negative thoughts or distractions come, we acknowledge them and then, as Byron Nelson said, "set them aside."

We've had hundreds of patients at our clinics, and the ones who do well after they leave are the ones who concentrate on the program that we design together with them.

Quite often I feel like I'm going in a million different directions. That feeling is depressive and self-defeating. But when it comes, I tell myself I have a choice: I can go on in my scatterbrained fashion, or I can decide right now that I'm going to focus on a particular matter for a certain amount of time.

I've written scores of books. I have a large medical practice. How can I write so many books and keep up with my responsibilities as a doctor?

I concentrate.

I take blocks of time and do nothing else but grind out pages on my computer. Sometimes it's only an hour or less. Sometimes it's four hours. But I concentrate.

I'm not naturally focused; I'm prone to wander. But when I tell myself that I can choose to stay focused for a certain amount of time, I find most often that I can.

The Bible offers a word of encouragement on this subject: "Let's not get tired of doing what is good. At just the right time we will reap a harvest of blessing if we don't give up."[13] When we set worthwhile goals—goals of improving our education, our relationships, or our spiritual life; goals of helping others; goals of serving God—we will reap benefits when we concentrate long enough to achieve them. Sometimes we get tired, but if we keep our goals in mind, we won't give up.

I've never been a golf champion. But if I can concentrate, I believe you can. It begins with a choice. Make the choice to concentrate upon what you feel is important to you, and you'll be making the choice of champions.

Three things Byron Nelson and Larry Nelson did to become champions

1. They concentrated on the immediate task before them, deliberately shutting out all distractions.
2. When distractions or negative thoughts occurred, they quickly dismissed them. They refused to concern themselves with what happened in the past or what might happen in the future.
3. They immersed themselves in a brief capsule of time in order to best execute the shot in front of them.

DAILY AFFIRMATION

I choose to concentrate on the next thing I need to do to meet my goals.

9

BONDO'S STORY

Champions Choose to Seek a Higher Purpose

The year: 1957.

The place: Scioto Country Club, Columbus, Ohio.

The players: Two nineteen-year-old junior golf champions. Big two hundred pounders. Young men who could pound a Titleist a mile.

Jack, the better known of the two, teed off first. Even though he had beaten all the PGA pros and won the state open and was recognized as the nation's top junior, he knew he would need his best game to beat Paul, who possessed a golf swing that was as pure and powerful as Sam Snead's.

Jack's backswing was upright. As he wound up, his left heel lifted completely off the ground. His right elbow flew skyward. He paused at the apex of his swing for a mere second. Then suddenly, he dropped his left heel to the ground. The force of Jack's downswing was so powerful that Paul, standing fourteen feet behind him and out of Jack's sight, heard his foot stomp the ground. The bowing shaft drove down with lightning speed. Paul's head snapped to his right as Jack rocketed his ball more than three hundred yards down the fairway.

"Good shot," Paul said, all the time planning to drive a few yards farther, no matter how far Jack hit it.

Paul set his mind on a slow, long swing. He realized he must drive accurately, too, because Jack's ball was right in the middle of the fairway.

The big blonds would play nine holes. Seven of these holes would be driving contests.

Paul glanced at Jack just as he addressed his drive. He wanted to make sure Jack was watching. He waggled his club twice and then took the club back in a slow, wide arc. But unlike Jack, he had no pause at the top of his backswing. Paul's swing resembled a long, lethal snap of a sixteen-foot leather whip. It seemed effortless, but by the time the club-head reached the ball, there was a loud crack.

The two boys eyed Paul's ball flying through the air. It landed twenty yards short of Jack's ball, bounced high, and rolled five yards farther.

Paul glanced toward Jack again. Paul smiled.

Jack smiled back.

Paul usually outdrove Jack, although Paul believed Jack might be stronger physically.

"Good shot," Jack said. Jack loved this. They had played three times together this week. In all three rounds, both of them scored under par. Most of the time only one shot separated them.

Today would be another tough test.

When the two juniors played, it was all business. Neither of them talked a lot. But on occasion, like today, they joked with each other.

Jack Grout, the head pro and instructor for both of the boys, sent them out on the back nine and told them to keep out of the way of members, who were accustomed to playing the front nine during the late afternoon.

Both parred the tenth hole.

On the eleventh, a par five, Jack drove first. He placed his shot directly in the middle of the fairway. Paul pulled his drive into the fairway bunker on the left. Jack again played first and put his three wood shot in front of the green.

Though Paul was more than 250 yards away from the green, he believed he was within reach. But only one club would get there: his three wood.

When Jack saw Paul pull his three wood out of his bag, he shook his head. He was thinking no one alive could hit a three wood out of this steep-faced bunker.

Paul saw things differently.

The ball was sitting up like it was on grass. He was sure he could pull off the shot. Taking no time, he placed his feet in the sand, waggled the club, and fired the ball out of the sand like a cannon ball.

Jack closed his eyes in disbelief.

The ball ripped through the air, but its trajectory was too low. It banged into the heavy grass lip of the bunker and rocketed into the sky.

Jack watched it arch twenty feet in the air and begin to fall in Paul's direction. Paul couldn't see it.

"Watch out!" Jack yelled. Too late. The ball landed squarely on Paul's head.

Jack broke out in laughter.

Paul gripped his head. It hurt. He glanced toward Jack, who was breaking up. Paul started laughing.

Jack shot two under that day, but after Paul's bean on the head and bogey on the hole, he birdied four holes and edged out his buddy—33 for Paul, 34 for Jack.

It was the fall of 1957 now. Paul Bondeson lost his golf companion, as Jack received a golf scholarship to Ohio State University. Jack and Jack's dad wanted Paul at Ohio State too.

But Paul wasn't about to go to college. He had other dreams. He wanted to be an actor, a dream he'd had since preteen days.

After the golf season ended, Paul left Columbus and trekked to New York City. He found a place to stay in Greenwich Village and met some famous actors. One was Robert Redford.

Two years passed.

June 1959. The U.S. Open was being held at Winged Foot Golf Club not far from where Paul was living in New York. Paul had played very little golf since Jack began at Ohio State.

Jack had steadily improved and had become golf's top collegiate player.

Paul, on the other hand, had learned about the effects of alcohol and drugs, the experience of being penniless and homeless, and the reality that acting was taking him nowhere.

Paul wanted to see Jack again, but he didn't want Jack to see him in his current state. So he disguised himself with sunglasses, a wide-brimmed hat, and a London Fog trench coat. He took the train north to Westchester.

He found Jack on the course and hid amidst the gallery. "He's improved," Paul whispered to himself. "He's better than ever."

On the eleventh hole, Paul walked closer to the fairway. Just then Jack glanced toward the gallery. Their eyes met.

Immediately, Paul dropped his head and backed away. *I hope to God he didn't see me like this,* Paul thought to himself. But he feared it was too late. An hour later he was back on the train heading into the city.

Two more years passed. Paul's mom came back into his life and persuaded him to commit himself to drug rehabilitation at Chattahoochee Mental Hospital in the northwest panhandle of Florida, not far from her home.

Not long after, one of the counselors found out about Paul's golf skills and made playing on the nine-hole course adjacent to the hospital part of his therapy. Soon his swing began to take shape. Getting back into golf loosened the grip that drugs and alcohol had on him.

When he was released, he began to practice daily. Within six months, he believed he was ready to compete against the top professionals in the world. His high school friend, Jack Nicklaus, had completed his four years at Ohio State and was preparing for the PGA Tour, too.

In just the sixth PGA event of 1962, Paul caught fire, inspired in part by playing a practice round with his childhood idol Ben Hogan, and tied Bob Goalby for the lead after fifty-four holes. That Saturday night he stayed up until 5 a.m. partying.

On that Sunday Paul was paired with Billy Casper in the final group. Jack Nicklaus was three shots back and playing in the second-to-last group. After ten holes, Paul led the tournament by three shots.

"I thought I was invincible," Paul says now. "The eleventh was 380 yards, playing downwind. I thought I could drive the green, and I did. Rolled it almost right between Nicklaus's legs." Paul two-putted for a birdie. With seven holes to play, he held a solid four-shot lead.

"Then my head started telling me, *You don't deserve to win*," Paul said. "*You're a drunk. Anyone who stays up all night drinking doesn't deserve to win.*"

On the twelfth, a par-five hole usually unreachable in two, Paul pulled his tee shot into the bunker. "The lip in front of me wasn't high," Paul recalls. "I thought I could reach the green, so I chose one of my favorite clubs—a one iron.

"I mashed it, but it came out low and buried under the top edge of the bunker. The sand nearly covered the ball. I was lucky just to get it out, and I ended up with a double bogey, which I followed up with another double on the thirteenth. My four-shot lead was gone.

"I settled down and parred fourteen, fifteen, sixteen, and seventeen, but Casper had me by a shot as we teed off on eighteen.

"I hit a big drive and had a nine iron to the green. Casper needed a wood on his second, hit a good shot, and made a par.

I needed a birdie to tie. I played my nine iron to within ten feet of the hole. I thought I could make this putt. When it was a couple of inches from the hole it was dead center. But at the last second it dipped down into the hole and lipped out.

"I couldn't believe it. But when I opened my eyes I could believe it. 'I didn't deserve to win.'

"I finished second. Nicklaus third. Ben Hogan fourth."

Though it was a tough loss, it was Paul's best tournament ever. Ben Hogan offered him a contract to play his new clubs, and MacGregor offered five times Hogan's offer. Paul's sponsors wanted him with MacGregor, and Paul conceded. "Another bad choice," Paul said later. "I let my sponsors make the decision. Maybe if I'd gone with Hogan he'd have helped me be a better player and person. I'll never know."

"I never could shake drinking," he says now. "I drank myself off Tour. I became an accident ready to happen."

That accident would happen. But first his addiction to alcohol would plummet him from the glamour of his six years on the PGA Tour to cutting the grass where the tournaments were played.

Though sponsors and media said a great talent had fallen, Paul saw it as a step out of the high-stress life on the PGA Tour, which fueled his craving for alcohol. Now he was free to be at home with his wife, Shirley, and their three children.

★

Paul was now a greenskeeper. His longtime friend Babe His-key, my brother and three-time PGA Tour winner, found him a job at Eldorado Country Club. Paul hadn't played—nor had he missed playing—the PGA Tour for two decades. The days he did play he still broke par. But most folks around Eldorado CC didn't know that.

One day Babe rolled out to the maintenance shed on a golf cart, looking for his friend. He found Paul back in the evergreen woods next to the shed, watching one lone golfer grinding on the practice range.

"What are you doing out here?" Babe said.

Paul shook his head and smiled. "Hi, Babe, look at one of my golf buddies over there. He can't get the ball airborne."

Babe turned his head and saw a man wearing a beret-style cap.

Babe waved Paul over to sit down on the golf cart. They watched the man struggle on four shots in succession. "He's so far ahead of the ball," Babe said. "It's either going to right field or low."

Paul nodded in agreement, his face grimacing.

"I can't stand it," Paul said. "Let's go over there. He might hurt himself."

Babe laughed and then drove them to the back side of the range. Paul jumped off the cart and sprinted onto the practice tee toward the man.

"William, I've been watching you," Paul said to his friend. "You're never going to hit that ball higher than your head if you don't learn a couple of things. Let me have that club."

William looked at Paul, his eyes wide and mouth open. He surrendered the club to Paul. "Okay," he said, "you show me."

"What is this?"

"Nine iron."

"William, you're the greatest. Nobody in the world would be out here on a hot day perfecting a shot like yours. I have to hand it to you. You're a hard worker."

"You got some idea how to hit it higher?"

Paul gripped the iron and faced William. "You have to move the ball forward in your stance. You're playing it off your right foot."

William wagged his head in a circle, bewildered. Paul used the clubhead to position the forty-compression range ball near his left heel. Paul's feet were thirty inches apart. He bowed slightly as he placed the clubhead behind the ball.

"Play the ball more toward the left foot when you want it to go high. And if you want to hit it real high, move it farther toward your left toe." Paul bumped the ball into place. He stood with his back to the range as he spoke to William. "You see the ninth green?" Paul pointed the shaft of his club toward it.

A grove of huge evergreens, the height of a ten-story building, blocked the view of the green.

"Yes, sir, I can see it," William said, leaning sideways to find the flag on the green, which was 150 yards away.

"Look up there," Paul said, pointing his club at the top of the trees.

Paul waggled the iron in his hands, then took a silky, wide-arc swing and sent the ball straight up like a bazooka.

William gazed upward. For a few moments there was silence. William's eyes were glued to the towering, rainbow flight of the ball.

His jaw dropped as the ball cleared the grove. His head started to shake back and forth. His mouth widened. Suddenly, he jumped sideways so he could see the green.

"The ball's on the green!" he shouted. "Ain't a man alive can do that. Why aren't you playing the Tour?"

Paul smiled. "I like being here better," he said. He laughed and walked back to sit by Babe, who was watching from the cart.

"You're unbelievable, Bondo," Babe said.

"Life improved when I moved to Houston," Paul said. "I had quit drinking many times before. I'd be sober six months then start drinking again. Babe Hiskey saved my life. I tried to shake him, but he'd always show up, no matter how bad the shape I was in. Babe had led me to Jesus Christ about the time we started a Bible study on the PGA Tour, but it wasn't until he got me to Houston, into the Bible and a good environment, that I really changed."

In their years in Houston and later in Florida, Paul and Shirley watched their children grow up, made some good investments, and even bought a home in the mountains near Murphy, North Carolina, where they planned to retire.

One weekend in 2001 while they were in Murphy, Paul was driving to the local middle school carnival to support a fund-raising event.

"The highway into Murphy is four lanes, with a median in between the eastbound and westbound lanes," Paul said. "A woman driving an old car decided to make a left turn. Didn't see us and crashed into the right side of our car. Instinctively, I threw my body over Shirley."

The crushing force of the collision catapulted their car into the air and sent it rolling over and over, knocking Paul unconscious. His body was pinned between the dashboard and the seat. Shirley, bloody and battered, escaped.

Paul had to be cut from the car.

He awakened two days later in the hospital in Murphy. He could not move anything or feel anything except his head. His doctor informed him his head was locked in a halo—a steel band the width of his forehead, which was wound around the top of his head. His spinal cord had been severed.

Through no fault of his own, Paul was now a quadriplegic. He would never drive a car again. Never walk. Never play golf. Shirley would have to bathe, dress, and feed him.

Shortly thereafter Babe called me and said that he, Chi Chi Rodriguez, Gary Player, and twenty other pros were holding a fund-raiser to help Paul with mounting medical bills.

"When you see Paul, you're going to be surprised," Babe told me. His question made me curious.

"Because he's totally paralyzed?" I asked.

"No. It's his face."

"What about his face?"

"He's got a perpetual smile," Babe said. "It's the most amazing thing I've ever seen. He never stops smiling."

A month later I arrived at the Palm Cove Golf and Yacht Club in south Florida just as Shirley was helping Paul get out of their van into his motorized wheelchair.

"Jimmy Hiskey." Paul's cheeks were pink, and he was smiling just as Babe had described. "Thanks for coming. Isn't this great, having everyone here?"

"Everyone loves you, Paul," I said, stunned by his bright countenance. It was so noticeable that I almost ignored his lifeless body. I walked beside him as he motored himself toward the front door of the sprawling clubhouse.

"I can't get over this," Paul said, "all these guys coming down here. Your brother, Chi Chi, Gary Player. It's just great. You know, Jimmy, some of us learn easy, but God had to hit me with a two-by-four to get my attention."

The next day I got together with Paul and Shirley at the golf range after the players teed off. It was a bright, sunny day. The Florida palm trees were swaying in the warm breeze.

I felt myself smile as I walked up to Paul. But I caught myself. *Paul is paralyzed,* I thought. *He's helpless. You should be feeling sad.*

"Hey, Jimmy, great to see you." He was beaming with joy. Shirley was sitting on a folding chair next to him.

I pulled up another chair facing them. We chatted about some memories of when we were both on the Tour.

I was eager to find out more about his longtime friendship with Jack Nicklaus. I asked, "Is it true that Jack said, 'If Paul Bondeson could have ridded himself of his demons, I'd never have had the record I had'?"

Paul laughed. "I've heard that."

"Babe tells me you have a perpetual smile," I said. "You never smiled like this when you were playing the Tour."

"I was an accident waiting to happen, Jimmy."

"What do you mean?"

"I mean I never felt like I deserved to be a success. I'd been a drunk, and if it wasn't for this woman who stuck with me through it all—" his eyes rolled to Shirley—"I wouldn't even be alive today."

Shirley nodded and smiled.

"I was lucky," he said. "If the police hadn't gotten there quickly, called an ambulance, and cut me out of the car, I'd never have made it."

"Did you ever wish that you hadn't?" I asked.

"The first thing I remember thinking after waking up was, 'The Lord giveth and the Lord taketh away. Blessed be the name of the Lord.' I don't think I've ever been depressed or wished I'd died."

I leaned back. I could hardly believe what I was hearing.

"For a while I wasn't sure I would live, but it didn't matter. Either way, I felt I had a great future. I knew God had a purpose for me."

"You saw a silver lining in the accident, and that's why you're smiling?"

Reading about Jim's friend Paul Bondeson has reaffirmed my belief that his life's purpose is not about gaining the most glory, fame, money, or recognition. Paul Bondeson's life began to change when he stepped back from the Tour and took a position as a humble greenskeeper. He dedicated himself to his family, became more serious about his faith, and worried less about himself and more about others.

Even after his accident, Paul wasn't depressed because he understood that God held his future. God had a purpose for his life. If Paul needed to fulfill that purpose while paralyzed, that was okay. He would trust God's judgment.

I never dreamed that God had a purpose for my life. My parents were German immigrants. Mom had only a third-grade education, and she worked as a maid for a couple of physicians. My dad was a carpenter, and I planned to follow in his footsteps. But at age sixteen, I did have a dream, in fact, two intense dreams the same night. In the first, Jesus, whom I knew very little about, appeared to me. He told me to become a doctor. I woke up from the dream so sure it was really from God that I said yes.

In the second dream I was a man in my forties. I was traveling from country to country. I taught practical living techniques, including spirituality, to people from many nations. I woke from that dream not knowing exactly what to do, but I decided to keep my mind open to being a missionary doctor like Albert Schweitzer.

These were risky goals for someone who had never tried hard in school and whose parents hadn't gone to college. Just like the adjustments I later made to my golf swing, I had to make multiple changes in my learning habits and attitudes. I had to overcome some obstacles to accomplish this purpose I felt God was giving me.

I fulfilled the first dream by becoming a medical doctor with five different academic degrees, including biology, cardiovascular physiology, medicine, psychiatry, and theology.

When I finished my psychiatric training at Duke University Medical Center, I turned down a high-paying job and instead taught first at Trinity Seminary in Deerfield, Illinois, and then at Dallas Theological Seminary. I taught full-time for less than 10 percent of what I would have made at the other jobs I was offered. But I felt the call from those dreams fifteen years earlier, and I knew I could do more good training multiple counselors than I could being a single therapist myself. I recognized the gifts God had given me, and I was happy to be able to use them for others.

Among my first students were Abede Alexandre, a Haitian student who later taught at Harvard; Tony Evans, an African-American student who became one of the most outstanding pastors and authors in America; John Trent; John Townsend; Henry Cloud; Dale Burke; Graham Barker; and other champions of the faith who have gone on to be some of the best psychologists, pastors, and authors in America.

Then a strange thing happened to me.

In the 1970s, almost no books integrated psychiatry and psychology with spirituality. In fact, many psychiatrists at the time belittled religious beliefs, which they defined as a "rubber crutch." So I wrote a book for each course I taught. The books sold well, and I ended up writing more books that were read by more people in more languages than I ever dreamed of.

Eventually I fulfilled my second dream by becoming an international traveler and teacher. It started in 1992, when

I went to Israel for the first of five trips to write novels about the Middle East.

On my way home, I was quite bored and lonely. So in Paris, before I got on board the plane to Chicago, I prayed, "Dear God, please put me beside someone who speaks English. If I don't get to talk to anyone for eleven straight hours, I will probably go nuts! Amen."

I boarded the plane, and a lovely thirty-year-old woman from Paris sat beside me. She spoke pretty good English, so I again said a silent prayer. "Thank you, Lord. She will do just fine. Help me to focus on her soul rather than her lovely face and body. Amen."

We began talking to each other without mentioning our names, and she told me that she had been very depressed at age twenty, in college in Paris. An American missionary had given her a book called *Happiness Is a Choice* by Drs. Paul Meier and Frank Minirth. She asked me if I was familiar with it.

"Why, yes," I said, trying not to show my utter surprise. "I have heard of it."

She said it had helped her overcome her severe depression, and now she herself had become a missionary to help college kids develop a relationship with God. But many of the students she was trying to help had serious problems, such as bulimia.

She said she was going to America not only to visit the woman who had given her the book but also to "hunt down" Dr. Paul Meier.

Astounded, I asked her, "And why do you want to hunt down Dr. Meier?"

"Because," she replied, "other missionaries and therapists in the Paris area want me to ask Dr. Meier how we can get more training in integrating the spiritual with the emotional and physical in counseling."

"I am Dr. Paul Meier," I said calmly. "When would you like me to come and train you and your friends?" At first Katherine did not believe me. But a few months later I was in France, training professional therapists, pastors, and missionaries.

Finally, I knew what God had meant when he gave me that second dream at age sixteen. Since that time, I've had the privilege of being on *Oprah* and many other TV and radio programs internationally, on which I've been heard by millions of people. I have trained thousands of physicians, psychiatrists, pastors, and missionaries in many nations.

I still have obstacles, not in any degree like those of Paul Bondeson, but they are still handicaps. One is attention deficit disorder (ADD). In some fields of medicine I'd be a danger. However, I take medication and in psychiatry I do well. I have a number of clinics and a staff of two hundred therapists. Like Paul Bondeson I've sought a higher purpose, and fortunately I have bypassed my handicaps. I love knowing that I'm contributing, that I'm helping others by the work that I do.

As I conclude this chapter, I want to chat with you as a doctor. Please imagine yourself sitting with me in my office.

I want to speak to you heart-to-heart for a few moments. In my mind, whether in golf or academics, each of us can become a champion if we overcome our obstacles and improve our lives. I like to think that champions are those who discover their God-given gifts and use them to the best of their ability—to benefit others.

By God's grace and leading, maybe I've become a champion in my field. If I can, I believe you can too, no matter what your gifts or what barriers you face.

Jim and I believe God has a purpose for each of us.

In the book of Jeremiah we read, "'For I know the plans I have for you,' declares the LORD, 'plans to prosper you and not to harm you, plans to give you a hope and a future.'"[14] God may not tell you your specific life purpose in a dream like he did for me. But you can be sure that the "hope and . . . future" he wants for you includes overcoming any obstacles that get in the way of living a healthy life. None could be more difficult than that of Paul Bondeson or Rachel or Cynthia Rowland, whom I will tell you more about in our last chapter.

Jesus himself said, "My purpose is to give . . . a rich and satisfying life."[15] He wants you to live life abundantly. We are convinced that he wants you to become a champion, and he can help you change your life.

Ordinary people *can* be champions. Champions get better at life. Your life *can* change. It may involve taking a risk, like Tiger did when he got a new golf doctor and a new plan for improvement, but you can be a champion in what matters most to you. You *can* find meaning and progress.

You *can* be sure God has a hope and a future for you. He will help you overcome obstacles and follow his higher purpose.

In the book of 2 Corinthians, the apostle Paul wrote about his own struggles with a "thorn in [the] flesh."[16]

We don't know whether this was a physical problem, a recurring sin, or something else. But when Paul prayed that it would be removed, the Lord answered, "'My grace is sufficient for you, for my power is made perfect in weakness.'"[17]

God's purpose for our lives doesn't require us to be perfect. Thank God for that!

Only he is perfect. Instead, to fulfill God's higher purpose for our lives, we need first to trust him. Trust that he has us right where we are in life for a purpose. Trust him even when we don't think we have much to offer. Trust that he knows best.

When we do that, we'll have a compass for our lives— and God's amazing peace besides.

Three things Paul Bondeson did to become a champion
1. He knew his shortcomings and learned to accept, not deny them. After many struggles, he realized that he couldn't stay on the Tour and maintain a healthy life. He gave up glamour for stability and peace.

2. He was humble. He didn't flaunt his unusual talent for golf but used it to help others.
3. He trusted in God's purpose, even when his life took unexpected turns. He believed that God could use him, regardless of the circumstances.

DAILY AFFIRMATION

I choose to believe that God has a higher purpose for my life. I choose to trust that he knows best and will lead me into that higher purpose.

10

THE CYNTHIA ROWLAND McCLURE STORY

The Ultimate Aim of a Champion

The great champions in sports aim to be the best.

Jack Nicklaus did it by winning more major championships than anyone who ever lived.

Tiger Woods became the best player in the world by holding the titles of all four major championships in a twelve-month span. He claimed the number-one ranking for eight of his first ten years as a professional golfer.

Michael Jordan became the best by retiring with the NBA's highest scoring average and leading his team to six NBA championships.

Lance Armstrong did it by winning the Tour de France seven consecutive times.

I love watching sports. But after counseling thousands of people, many very successful in their fields, I've found that athletic, financial, career, or political success does not satisfy the deepest longing of the human heart.

One of our most renowned psychologists, Abraham Maslow, did extensive research on basic human needs, establishing what we now refer to as Maslow's hierarchy of needs. Briefly stated, Maslow's studies show us that after people satisfy their physiological needs as well as their needs for safety and security, love, and belonging, they desire to fulfill *esteem needs*—status, recognition, appreciation, and dignity.

But there is one more need that he says transcends all the others: *self-actualization*. Esteem needs are more outward and connected with the *doing* of life, but self-actualization is inward and related to the *being* of life. It has to do with fulfilling our potential and purpose and becoming everything we're capable of. Maslow says it is only by meeting this need that we can be our "fullest."

Jim and I believe that this highest need comes from the fact that we are created beings. We believe we are created for a higher purpose, and to fulfill this highest of all needs we must seek him to find out why we've been created.

Jim and I have one major thing in common. We both love golf.

There's also one thing we don't have in common: skill. He's skilled at playing golf. I am skilled in watching it on Sunday afternoons.

But there's another, more important thing we have in common: a rock-solid belief that we've been created with purpose.

Our overall purpose as humans is to be in relationship with God through Jesus Christ. But God also has given each of us gifts, and he wants us to use them. He has a specific purpose for each of us individually. We believe the discovery of that purpose can bring a person to the highest level of joy and meaning in life.

In an earlier chapter, I told you about one of the greatest champions who has ever been to one of our clinics—Cynthia Rowland. Suicidal and desperately struggling with bulimia, she sought help, accepted her past mistakes, got up, and moved on.

I only told you part of her story.

The day she said good-bye to us in Dallas, I assumed she would go back into television broadcasting. She was beautiful. Young. Light, golden hair. Bright eyes. A big smile. A wrinkleless face.

Cynthia had experienced success in her years of broadcasting before we met. When she left Dallas, she had a choice. She could capitalize on her talent, which would provide considerable recognition and financial benefits. Or she could dedicate herself to helping those who, like herself, were suffering from various food addictions.

Cynthia chose the latter. She chose a higher purpose, something she believed was more significant than television. Cynthia believed she'd been cured of an incurable disease and could not remain quiet about it. I felt honored when she asked me if I would be a coauthor of her book, *The Monster Within*, now in its sixteenth or seventeenth printing. She also began to tell her story publicly. When she did, listeners were moved.

Phones at our clinic started ringing. People with eating problems were calling.

Broadcasting had lost its appeal to Cynthia. She couldn't feel at home in broadcasting when millions of people were suffering from food addictions, living secret lives.

I don't know how or when she discovered it, but a quote by the apostle Paul became her life maxim: "Praise be to the God and Father of our Lord Jesus Christ, the Father of compassion and the God of all comfort, who comforts us in all our troubles, so that we can comfort those in any trouble with the comfort we ourselves have received from God."[18]

After *The Monster Within* hit bookstores, Cynthia began a new life. She founded and began to grow her not-for-profit organization, Hope for the Hungry Heart, designed to bring hope and comfort to those suffering with food addictions.

Cynthia never did anything half-throttle. She became a motivational speaker, and doors opened for her to speak all across the United States. For two years, she completely immersed herself in her mission.

I frequently expected one of my non-Christian psychiatrist friends to call me and say that my patient Cynthia had not been healed of addiction, but had only substituted a religious addiction for her food. I never got the call, but I had my answer prepared. "Except for two things," I would say. "She's saved the lives of several young women, and she laughs."

Cynthia laughed a lot. I admit I had some concern when she seemed to sacrifice her career and just about everything else for her new life. But what I like to see in my patients is a capacity to laugh at themselves. She did.

She tells one story that happened right after we finished *The Monster Within.*

She was speaking at a large conference in Colorado. She had a role reversal. Instead of *doing* the interview, as she had in her broadcasting days, she was the one *being* interviewed.

The interviewer asked her, "Cynthia, are you married?"

"No," she said. "I was married when I was nineteen and divorced at nineteen."

"Will you ever marry again?"

"I don't think so."

"Why?"

"I've given my singleness to God, and I don't think he wants me to marry."

No one questioned Cynthia's total dedication to her cause.

She later told me, "One hour later I was trying to walk through a crowded hallway, and I bumped into this man almost head-on. So close our name tags pinned together. We laughed and tried to get untangled, both embarrassed. Yet we were strangely attracted to each other.

"A year later I married that man. I laugh now. I think God must have been laughing when he heard me pontificating in the interview about how I would never marry."

Her marriage nearly didn't happen.

She fell in love with the same enthusiasm she did everything else in life. When she fell for David McClure, she was consumed by him. All she thought about was this marvelous man that God had been keeping for her.

David's passion for Cynthia was the same. "We became soul mates," David says now.

During their courtship, Cynthia was living in Oklahoma City and David in Los Angeles. One day she noticed a bulge the size of a marble on her left breast. At first she didn't tell David; she didn't want him to worry. She hurried to a doctor, who assured her that it was only a cyst and told her not to worry about it. Her mother insisted that she get a second opinion. She did and found out it was breast cancer. If it wasn't removed immediately, she might die.

Cynthia had faced death many times before she came to Dallas.

She didn't want to die. She didn't want to lose David. But she didn't want David to live his life around the care of a cancer patient. She loved him too much for that.

When she told David she didn't want to lose her breast, he assured her of his love and the necessity of the surgery.

A week later her left breast was removed. The doctors said the cancer had all been extracted and gave the soon-to-be-married couple high hopes for the future.

A few months later Cynthia became Mrs. David Mc-Clure.

David encouraged Cynthia to continue her work with Hope for the Hungry Heart. She did it with as much fervor as ever. But something was missing in Cynthia's life. Something both Cynthia and David deeply desired: children.

However, the doctor who had operated on her, as well as two other doctors whom Cynthia and David consulted, told them that her cancer was estrogen receptive. If she became pregnant, there was a good chance it would ignite any cancer that might be in her body.

Another heartbreak for Cynthia.

But like all great champions, Cynthia chose to get back up again. She accepted her cancer-produced barrenness and poured herself back into her work.

Four and a half years passed. Though the cancer had disappeared, her heart to be a mother had not.

One evening the two thirty-five-year-olds decided to pray.

"We took a walk," David said. "We said a short prayer. 'Dear Lord, we'd sure love to have a little baby. Please send one our way if it's okay with you. In Jesus' name, amen.'"

Cynthia had one condition to adoption: She wanted to know the child's mother.

Unexpectedly, the next day, Cynthia received a call from a single mother-to-be from Canada. The young woman had read Cynthia's book and was looking for a family for her expected baby.

"She called *me* for help," Cynthia told David, laughing. "She's already interviewed several couples but she wants *us* to take her baby."

Later that year Cynthia and David met Laraine to discuss the plan more fully. They fell in love with each other. Cynthia asked Laraine if she wanted to move to Los Angeles to live with them and have the baby there. Laraine accepted. Because Cynthia's book had been a lifesaver to Laraine, she was happy to do for Cynthia what Cynthia could not do for herself.

Soon Micah, "the most beautiful baby ever born," became Cynthia and David's son.

Not long after, Cynthia went back to her doctor for a routine annual checkup. The cancer cut from her body had been eliminated for five years. There were no traces of new cancer. The report was good. She was "cancer free."

David and Cynthia celebrated.

They decided to adopt again. Another boy, Caleb.

Cynthia was happier than any time in her life. She was married to the greatest man on earth. She had two of the greatest little boys in the world, and she was helping to save the lives of many young women imprisoned by food addictions.

On a morning when the October sky was a bright powder blue with not a cloud in sight, Cynthia's life darkened.

After Cynthia drove Micah to school, she dropped by her doctor's office for a routine checkup and went happily home.

The next day, her doctor called. "Cynthia, the cancer's back. It's spreading fast."

It was Friday. "They want to start chemo on Monday," she told David.

Two weeks later, her blonde hair was almost gone. More chemo. Then a bone marrow transplant. Everything was failing.

But Cynthia kept speaking to groups. Inside she believed she was dying. She began producing a video that she hoped would be a legacy to David and her boys.

She lost all her hair. David tried to cheer her up by calling her his "bald chick."

They prayed for a miracle. They prayed the cancer would go into remission. But things worsened.

She decided to tell Micah, now seven, and Caleb, six, that she would soon die.

After an early evening speaking engagement, she returned home wearing a full wig, spiked shoes, and long earrings that dangled below her chin. Her normal attire. She pulled off her shoes, stripped herself of her wig, and whispered to David, "I love you." He kissed her and whispered back, "You're some bald chick."

They called the boys into their bedroom and let them do what they loved to do—bounce on the bed.

Cynthia hugged them and retreated to David's arms. All four of them lay together snugly. She began to cry.

"Micah and Caleb, I need to tell you why I'm crying," she said, her voice breaking. They looked at her, their eyes soft and innocent.

Micah asked, "What's wrong, Mommy?"

"I'm crying because I am dying. I will be leaving you soon so I can be with Jesus in heaven."

She reached out and brought them into her embrace again, sobbing. "I'm making a movie for you and Daddy. I don't wear my wig. I'm the bald chick." She laughed half-heartedly. "In the movie I tell you all about my life from when I was little like you are, until today."

Large tears slid down her cheeks.

She began to wail.

David pulled her into his arms. A few moments passed.

"Do you understand?" she asked Micah.

"Yaaah," Micah answered. Caleb began to mimic his brother bouncing on the bed.

"Do you, Caleb?"

"Yaaah."

They didn't. But Cynthia smiled. She was at peace because she'd told them.

Some time later David McClure arranged another celebration for Cynthia. All her family arrived. Many friends.

Mike Moore, the doctor who first asked Cynthia, "When did you decide you were damaged freight?" and the person most responsible for her great success, spoke. David called the occasion "The Homegoing Celebration for Cynthia Rowland McClure."

"I have worked with terminally ill individuals for over twenty-five years," Mike said. "And I've never known anyone who integrated toughness and tenderness like Cynthia Rowland McClure.

"Her perception of Jesus expanded with her struggle with cancer. She simultaneously accepted the reality of her condition and maintained hope for healing.

"As she physically slowed down, she was vulnerable to discouragement and despair, yet she exerted every ounce of energy to persevere and hope against hope.

"She truly fought the good fight. . . ."

Cynthia Rowland McClure embodied all the choices of a champion.

Like Gary Player, she chose to focus on what was inside rather than the outside.

Like Tiger Woods, she risked change. She chose to come to our clinic to try to get well.

Like Betsy King, she accepted help from others.

Like Paul Hamm, she got up time and time again and moved on, writing a new script for her life.

Like Linda Armstrong Kelly, she found a way to turn her problems—her past experiences with bulimia—into opportunities to help others.

Like Lee Janzen and Bruce, she never gave up, even when facing serious illness and death.

Like Rachel, she faced the reality of her situation and made a plan to change.

Like Byron Nelson, she concentrated on that plan and the most significant things in her life.

And finally, like Paul Bondeson, she looked for her higher purpose. She found it in serving God, sharing her story, and helping others.

Cynthia was a winner, a true champion in life. She left her husband and two sons a great legacy. And she has left all of us who aspire to be champions in life a model to follow.

Some of Mike's words at Cynthia's funeral were an echo of the apostle Paul, one of the great champions of faith and the writer of half the books in the New Testament. Paul wrote this as he approached the end of his life: "I have fought the good fight, I have finished the race, and I have remained faithful."[19]

That's the epitaph of a champion.

Our hope is that you have been inspired by these stories. Some focus on incredible athletes, but many others describe ordinary people just like you and me. As they faced obstacles in their lives, they made the right choices—the choices of champions.

And so can you.

May these stories encourage you to take a step, set a goal, make the right choice . . . and be a champion in what matters most.

Choices of Champions

★ CHAMPIONS CHOOSE TO ACCEPT HELP FROM OTHERS.

★ CHAMPIONS CHOOSE TO RISK CHANGE.

★ CHAMPIONS CHOOSE TO GET UP AND MOVE ON.

★ CHAMPIONS CHOOSE TO FIND A WAY.

★ CHAMPIONS CHOOSE TO FACE THEIR PROBLEMS HEAD-ON.

★ CHAMPIONS CHOOSE TO PERSEVERE.

★ CHAMPIONS CHOOSE TO CONCENTRATE.

★ CHAMPIONS CHOOSE TO SEEK A HIGHER PURPOSE.

About the Authors

Jim Hiskey

Jim Hiskey grew up in southern Idaho. Because his father was a golf course superintendent, Jim and his two brothers learned to play golf at early ages.

Jim won more than thirty amateur and pro golf events as well as three Idaho State Amateur Championships before graduating from the University of Houston, where he was named all-American and played on three NCAA championship golf teams during the years 1956–1958.

Jim is a former PGA Tour player and instructor. He has been a golf pro since 1958 and presently is a life member of the PGA of America. He has given golf lessons to members of Congress and heads of state, including the secretary general of China and the president of Bangladesh. He has also instructed many pros on the PGA and Senior PGA Tours.

While competing on the PGA Tour, Jim coauthored the book *Golf How?* with former U.S. Open champion Orville Moody, and for eighteen years, he served as editor of *Links Letter*.

Jim was the cofounder of the PGA Tour Fellowship and served in the role of an informal chaplain for more than twenty-five years. He helped start the Champions

Tour Fellowship and the College Golf Fellowship, as well as Student Leadership, Cornerstone, and the C. S. Lewis Institute, which grew out of his forty-year association with the National Prayer Breakfast. He has also been working with professional golfers to establish fellowships in all forty-one sections of the PGA.

Jim and his wife, Lorraine, have been married for forty-eight years and live in Annapolis, Maryland. They are the parents of three children and the grandparents of eight.

Paul Meier

Dr. Paul Meier is a nationally recognized psychiatrist and founder of the Meier Clinics, a national chain of counseling and day-program facilities that employ 140 psychiatrists, psychologists, and therapists.

Dr. Meier has authored and coauthored more than seventy books, including *Love Is a Choice, Happiness Is a Choice, Unbreakable Bonds,* and *Blue Genes.* He has hosted a live, national talk radio program for twenty years and is a frequent guest on numerous radio and television programs, including *The Oprah Winfrey Show* and Joyce Meyer's *Enjoying Everyday Life.* In addition, he has been interviewed on Radio Free Europe and has appeared in a French television documentary discussing Christian psychiatry.

Acknowledged as a pioneer in the integration of psychological and spiritual dimensions with physical aspects, Dr. Meier has taught at many universities and seminaries throughout the world. A well-known national and international speaker, he lectures on insight-oriented therapy and other related topics. Dr. Meier has been a guest speaker for the past three years at Awakening, an annual weekend retreat for business and political leaders to exchange ideas, examine trends, and learn from leading authorities and policy makers in a variety of fields.

Dr. Meier also served as a member of the Dallas Mayor and Dallas County Judge's Health Alliance.

Dr. Meier received his master's degree in cardiovascular physiology from Michigan State University and a medical degree from the University of Arkansas College of Medicine in Little Rock. He completed his psychiatry residency at Duke University Medical Center. In 1984, he obtained another degree from Dallas Theological Seminary.

In addition to his busy speaking and writing schedule, Dr. Meier treats patients at the Meier Clinics Day Program in Richardson, Texas. The Meier Clinics can be contacted toll-free at (888) 7-CLINIC. Visit Dr. Meier's Web site at www.paulmeiermd.com.

Acknowledgments

Without the generosity of some capable people this book would not exist.

At the top of our list is Jim's wife, Lorraine, who has been with us since the first day we met. Lorraine, you have been a rock. Next, Dale Bowell, who read, reread, typed, and retyped repeatedly. Thank you, Dale. You are a champion. Thanks, too, to Dave, your loyal husband, for reading the manuscript and encouraging us along the way.

One special lady should not go unmentioned: our dear friend, Ella Webb. Without you, we would never have met. Thank you, Ella.

We are grateful to Lisa Jackson and Karin Buursma, our editors at Tyndale. Thanks, too, to Sharon Leavitt, Elizabeth Gosnell, Sarah Atkinson, Janis Harris, and the great team at Tyndale House for making this book possible. Special thanks to you, Lisa. You've been enjoyable to work with. If one life is changed as a result of this book, we will all rejoice. But it wouldn't have happened without your good suggestions and editing.

David McClure was an enormous help to us in bringing Cynthia Rowland McClure's story to life. Thank you, David, for materials you sent us and for your telephone interviews. You married a true champion.

Shirley Bondeson, loyal wife of Paul, and their daughters are true caregivers. They are heroes in our Hall of Champions. Thank you for wheeling Paul to us when we were together in Florida and for helping arrange the subsequent telephone calls, as well as for your dedication to Paul.

Many thanks to Jeff and Ken Hopper and the Links Players Team. Excerpts from the Bondo, Janzen, Nelson, and other stories ran first in *Links Letter* or on the Links Players Web page as daily devotionals.

We would also like to thank Paul Meier's personal assistant of twenty-three years, Carol Mandt, who has given editorial guidance and oversight to this and many of Paul's other books over the years. Her loving dedication to making sure that people receive the help they need and deserve through printed materials is greatly appreciated.

Thank you all.

Paul and Jim

Resources

Your heart may have been touched by some of the stories in this book, including that of Linda Armstrong Kelly, Paul Bondeson, or Cynthia Rowland McClure. If you would like to help them or learn more about their work, you may contact them at:

LANCE ARMSTRONG FOUNDATION
www.laf.org
(512) 236-8820

PAUL BONDESON
7643 S.E. Bay Cedar Circle
Hobe Sound, FL 33455

DAVID McCLURE
Hope for the Hungry Heart
Box 41
Chino Hills, CA 91707
E-mail: hope4heart@juno.com

You may also be interested in Linda Armstrong Kelly's book, *No Mountain High Enough* (available at www.lindaarmstrong.com) or Cynthia Rowland McClure's book *The Monster Within* (available through Fleming Revell/Baker Book House, Box 6287, Grand Rapids, MI 49516-6282).

Notes

1. Luke 10:41-42
2. James 5:16
3. Matthew 5:4
4. Proverbs 24:16
5. Some readers will be aware of the medal controversy that erupted soon after Paul Hamm's victory at the Olympics. The Korean bronze medalist's parallel bars routine was given a start value that was 0.1 too low. If that error had been caught in time, he would have won gold and Paul would have won silver. However, all the review panels agreed that Paul should keep the gold medal, and the scoring controversy certainly doesn't negate his incredible comeback.
6. Romans 3:23
7. Psalm 103:12
8. Linda Armstrong Kelly, *No Mountain High Enough* (New York: Random House, 2005), 181–82.
9. Psalm 32:5
10. John 8:36
11. Philippians 3:13-14
12. Hebrews 12:1-2
13. Galatians 6:9
14. Jeremiah 29:11, NIV
15. John 10:10
16. 2 Corinthians 12:7
17. 2 Corinthians 12:9, NIV
18. 2 Corinthians 1:3-4, NIV
19. 2 Timothy 4:7

the things your teachers never told you could be the most important things of all . . .

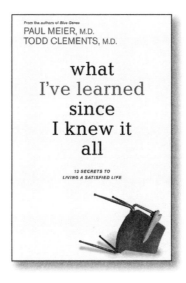

From the authors of *Blue Genes*
PAUL MEIER, M.D.
TODD CLEMENTS, M.D.

what
I've learned
since
I knew it
all

12 SECRETS TO
LIVING A SATISFIED LIFE

We may think we know it all, but even the best of us occasionally still need a few real-life lessons. In *What I've Learned Since I Knew It All*, psychiatrist and best-selling author Dr. Paul Meier teams up with Dr. Todd Clements to share what they have learned from their own mistakes and life experiences, as well as from decades of counseling patients who also thought they knew it all. This book lays out twelve crucial secrets to a satisfied life . . . and will teach you how to gain real success and happiness.

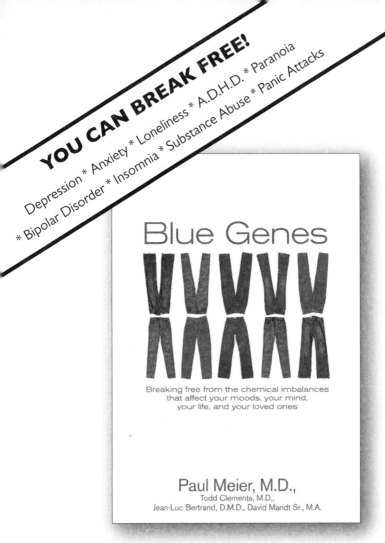

Blue Genes

Breaking free from the chemical imbalances
that affect your moods, your mind,
your life, and your loved ones

Paul Meier, M.D.,
Todd Clements, M.D.,
Jean-Luc Bertrand, D.M.D., David Mandt Sr., M.A.

Many common psychological problems, such as depression, bipolar disorder, obsessive-compulsive disorder, and A.D.H.D., can be linked to chemical imbalances in the brain. Paul Meier, M.D., whose clinic treats thousands of people per week, has written *Blue Genes* to help those who struggle find answers. Through fascinating case studies, Dr. Meier shows the dramatic difference that counseling and medicine can make. This empowering book addresses how genetics, environment, diet, fitness, and spirituality all affect our minds and our quality of life.

"IF COMPETITION WERE A VIRUS, WE WOULD HAVE AN EPIDEMIC ON OUR HANDS."

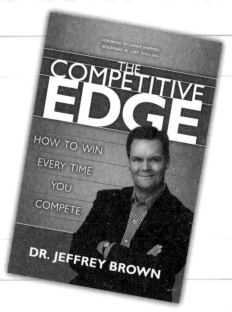

We all face competition every day, and we all want to win. But can you still be a serious competitor if you value qualities like character and integrity? Even better, can these attributes actually *help* you on your way to the top?

Clinical and sport psychologist Dr. Jeffrey Brown says that the answer is yes. Identifying seven crucial principles that will guide you to victory every time you compete, he'll teach you to recognize your successes, redefine what it means to be a winner, and develop a strong character that will truly give you a competitive edge in all of life's games.

CP0193